NEW DIRECTIONS FOR PROGRAM EVALUATION
A Publication of the American Evaluation Association

A D
17-12-90

Nick L. Smith, *Syracuse University*
EDITOR-IN-CHIEF

Advances in Program Theory

Leonard Bickman
Vanderbilt University

EDITOR

Number 47, Fall 1990

JOSSEY-BASS INC., PUBLISHERS
San Francisco

ADVANCES IN PROGRAM THEORY
Leonard Bickman (ed.)
New Directions for Program Evaluation, no. 47
Nick L. Smith, Editor-in-Chief

Microfilm copies of issues and articles are available in 16mm and 35mm,
as well as microfiche in 105mm, through University Microfilms Inc., 300
North Zeeb Road, Ann Arbor, Michigan 48106.

LC 85-644749   ISSN 0164-7989   ISBN 1-55542-813-4

NEW DIRECTIONS FOR PROGRAM EVALUATION is part of The Jossey-Bass
Higher and Adult Education and Social and Behavioral Science Series
and is published quarterly by Jossey-Bass Inc., Publishers (publication
number USPS 449-050).

EDITORIAL CORRESPONDENCE should be sent to the Editor-in-Chief,
Nick L. Smith, School of Education, Syracuse University, 330 Huntington
Hall, Syracuse, New York 13244-2340.

Printed on acid-free paper in the United States of America.

CONTENTS

EDITOR'S NOTES   1
Leonard Bickman

PART ONE: Conceptual Issues

1. Issues in Constructing Program Theory   7
Huey-tsyh Chen
Both normative and causative aspects of program theory are needed to
conduct evaluations.

2. Administrators as Applied Theorists   19
Charles McClintock
Effective administrators use theory in their roles as managers and leaders
in organizations.

PART TWO: Methodological Approaches

3. From Program Theory to Tests of Program Theory   37
Melvin M. Mark
Program theory needs to be tested in order to contribute to the field of
program evaluation.

4. Using Path Analysis to Develop and Evaluate Program Theory   53
and Impact
Nick L. Smith
Path analysis is an effective method for testing program theory.

PART THREE: Applications

5. Using Program Theory to Describe and Measure Program   61
Quality
Leonard Bickman, Keith A. Peterson
Program theory is a necessary ingredient in the development of measures
of program quality.

6. Developing and Testing Program Classification and Function   73
Theories
Kendon J. Conrad, Janet R. Buelow
The application of program theory to adult day care is described.

7. A Pattern-Matching Approach to Link Program Theory and   93
Evaluation Data
Jules M. Marquart
The utilization of a pattern-matching approach for developing and testing
program theory is discussed.

8. Linking Program Theory and Social Science Theory 109
Leslie J. C. Riggin
The ways in which social science theory can contribute to program theory
are demonstrated.

INDEX 121

EDITOR'S NOTES

The purpose of this volume is to further explore the role of program theory in program evaluation. In the more than two years since the publication of the first NDPE volume on this topic (Bickman, 1987), there have been a number of important milestones in the conceptualization of program theory: A number of panels at American Evaluation Association meetings have explored program theory, a book focusing on theory-driven evaluations has been published by Huey-tsyh Chen (1990), and a special issue of *Evaluation and Program Planning* (Chen, 1989) has been devoted to program theory. This all points to the increasing attention theory is receiving in the evaluation field. The development and utilization of program theory have importance not only to research-oriented evaluators but also to evaluation practitioners, program developers, administrators, and policymakers. It is hoped that increased emphasis on program theory will not only elevate the quality of evaluations but also develop stronger links between evaluations, program development, and policy.

This second volume, *Advances in Program Theory*, brings together three of the contributors to the previous series volume and five new authors. The authors illuminate new perspectives on program theory, review the development of innovative methodologies, and examine the use of program theory in the field. The volume is organized into three sections: conceptual issues, methodological approaches, and applications.

The first chapter, by Huey-tsyh Chen, amplifies the meaning of program theory by providing different explanations of the term "program theory." Chen emphasizes that most of the writers in this field conceptualize program theory as descriptive, that is, describing the program and how it works. Chen goes beyond this and suggests that program theory is also prescriptive, that is, it includes what the program should accomplish. This aspect of program theory is much more value-laden than the descriptive approach to program theory. Although valuing is implicitly a key aspect of evaluation, it has not received much attention. The dominance of method-driven evaluations may partially explain this gap. Chen argues that a theory-driven approach can also include social science approaches as well as stakeholder approaches. Chen provides a conceptualization that can guide evaluators in producing comprehensive program theory. This is an approach that promises to improve not only social programming but knowledge about social problems as well. One can see hints of delivery on this promise in the applications described by Bickman and Peterson, and Riggin in the last section in this volume.

In Chapter Two, Charles McClintock takes a different approach to conceptualizing program theory. This chapter describes a conceptual frame-

1

work that is derived from how administrators utilize information. In particular, McClintock conceives of applied program theory as a method of organizing knowledge in the service of action and as a way to acquire knowledge from action. The key is that administrators must engage in some action to improve programs. Based on five case studies, McClintock synthesized methods administrators used in applied theorizing. These strategies were then categorized into two broad dimensions of administrator action—management and leadership. These two dimensions are each subdivided into three different strategies that form the conceptual framework for understanding how administrators use information to improve programs. Understanding the basic dimensions of how administrators theorize about programs should help evaluators work with administrators to produce more relevant evaluations.

The next section of this volume deals with methodological approaches to program theory. Approaching the issue head on in Chapter Three, Melvin M. Mark takes the perspective that methods for testing program theory are critical if program theory is truly going to have an impact on the field of evaluation. In this chapter, Mark focuses on the development of methods for testing causal program theory. Some approaches described by Mark include causal modeling, multiple methodologies, and pattern matching. Mark carefully justifies the use of program theory to develop complex theoretical patterns that can then be compared to actual program data. He believes that these patterns help establish the causal relationship between the program's activities and its purported effects. Mark provides some very helpful methods for testing program theory, which, if carefully applied, will advance the field of evaluation. While each of these approaches has certain limitations, the combination of some of these methods should yield very robust tests of program theory.

In Chapter Four, Nick L. Smith provides a brief but comprehensive overview of path analysis as a way to explore causal theories. Smith notes the basic advantages of using this form of causal modeling but also provides some guidelines to prevent its misuse. As another tool in the program evaluator's assessment kit, path analysis should help advance the use of program theory.

The last section of this volume focuses on applications of program theory, illustrating how the theory can be used in the evaluation of both single projects and programs containing multiple sites or projects. Three of the applications (Bickman and Peterson, Conrad and Buelow, and Riggin) use multiple sites in their studies, while the other example in this section (Marquart) uses a single program. The applications provided are also from diverse fields, demonstrating the universal potential for productively using program theory.

The first chapter in this section, by Leonard Bickman and Keith A. Peterson, applies program theory to another relatively new concept in evaluation: quality. While there is significant contemporary interest in quality and its measurement outside of evaluation, there has been little development of this concept in the field of evaluation. As Bickman and Peterson point out, the utilization of quality has many potential advantages to evaluation, but its development has been retarded because it has been difficult to measure quality. They approach the measurement issue not from a methods perspective but rather from a program theory perspective. They illustrate the application of program theory to the measurement of quality in an evaluation of 175 preschool programs for handicapped children.

In an example from an evaluation of 74 adult day-care programs, Kendon J. Conrad and Janet R. Buelow also use program theory to develop measures of program characteristics. Using multiple stakeholders, they show in Chapter Six how their classification theory of programs was significantly related to client satisfaction. By using a large sample of projects, these investigators were able to develop a theoretically based classification scheme that helped predict client outcome.

In Chapter Seven, Jules M. Marquart uses pattern-matching theory to evaluate a child care program provided by a large employer. By pattern matching, Marquart means measuring the correspondence between the expected pattern of results or outcomes and the actually obtained pattern. In a clear and concise description she leads the reader through the steps that are necessary to conduct this type of evaluation. This approach holds great promise in its ability to provide greater confidence in evaluations that utilize nonrandomized designs. However, as Marquart points out, evaluation is very sensitive to the adequacy of the initial theory and the sensitivity of measurement.

In the final chapter, Leslie J. C. Riggin examines employment training for welfare recipients, also using the pattern-matching technique to evaluate the program's operation or implementation. She found that the evaluation uncovered new features that were not in the original program model. While the evaluation was useful both to the program administrators and to the evaluators, Riggin illustrates how the application of social science theory might have improved the evaluation. In particular, application of theories of compliance to the welfare recipients' behavior would have focused the data collection efforts and resulted in a better match between theory and outcome. Riggin also shows how social science theory can be used to strengthen the interpretation of evaluation results.

Program theory has the potential to increase the impact and quality of both programs and evaluations. In the long run, the better conceptualized and coherent programs will lead to evaluations that are better designed and have more impact. Program theory is one important road to this goal.

Leonard Bickman
Editor

References

Bickman, L. (ed.). *Using Program Theory in Evaluation.* New Directions for Program Evaluation, no. 33. San Francisco: Jossey-Bass, 1987.

Chen, H.-T. (ed.). Special issue on "The Theory-Driven Perspective." *Evaluation and Program Planning,* 1989, *12,* entire issue.

Chen, H.-T. *Theory-Driven Evaluations.* Newbury Park, Calif.: Sage, 1990.

Leonard Bickman is a professor of psychology, psychiatry, and public policy at Vanderbilt University, Nashville, Tennessee. He is director of the Program Evaluation Laboratory at Peabody College and director of the Mental Health Policy Center at the Vanderbilt Institute for Public Policy Studies.

PART ONE

Conceptual Issues

In designing theory-driven evaluations, it is important to understand
the normative and causative aspects of program theory, different
theory-construction approaches, the typology of theory-driven
evaluations, and analytical techniques for carrying out the
evaluations.

Issues in Constructing Program Theory

Huey-tsyh Chen

This chapter attempts to examine systematically the following fundamental issues related to integrating program theory into evaluation procedures. What is the nature of program theory? Are there different types of theory-driven evaluations for different purposes? How does one construct program theory?

The Nature of Program Theory

Social scientists usually define the term "theory" as a set of interrelated propositions that explain and predict a phenomenon (for example, Kerlinger, 1986). The definition, however, relates primarily to "descriptive theory" (Lave and March, 1975), which strives to analyze events as they actually are without suggesting how they ought to be. Rooted in the logical positivism advocated by philosophers of science such as Popper (1959) and Hemple (1965), descriptive theory has always dominated the social sciences and has had considerable influence on program evaluation. Contemporary program theory is essentially descriptive, focusing on describing or explaining facts and relationships. For example, Bickman (1987, p. 5) defines program theory as "the construction of a plausible and sensible model of how a program is supposed to work." Lipsey (1987, p. 7) defines program theory as "a set of propositions regarding what goes on in the black box during the transformation of input into output; that is, how, via

---

For a more detailed discussion of some of the issues raised in this chapter, see Chen (1990).

NEW DIRECTIONS FOR PROGRAM EVALUATION, no. 47, Fall 1990 ©Jossey-Bass Inc., Publishers

treatment inputs, a bad situation is transformed into a better one." Similarly, Wholey (1987, p. 78) argues that program theory identifies "program resources, program activities, and intended program outcomes, and specifies a chain of causal assumptions linking program resources, activities, intermediate outcomes, and ultimate goals."

Descriptive theory, however, is not the only type of theory that exists. Another type of theory that may be of relevance to program evaluation is "prescriptive theory." Prescriptive theory suggests what ought to be done or how to do something better. The rational decision model, which tells people how to make choices to maximize their expected utilities (Lave and March, 1975), is an example of prescriptive theory. Prescriptive theory recommends how people should behave in ideal circumstances and therefore makes explicit value judgments.

Since program evaluation involves not only describing what the program is but also suggesting what should be done, program theory needs to incorporate prescriptive theory as well as descriptive theory. The very selection of criteria for judging program performance involves value judgments. Issues such as how to design and implement the treatment are also value-laden. Prescriptive program theory includes the following dimensions: action orientation, conceptualization of treatment design and implementation, and selection of outcome criteria.

Action Orientation. Program theory examines specific strategies for achieving a goal or solving a social problem. These strategies imply that something needs to be done to improve a current situation. This concern with social action is basic to program evaluation and sets program theory apart from other, more descriptive, social theories.

The following example illustrates the difference between program theory and other social theories. Goode's (1971) resource theory identifies a husband's lack of resources (for example, income, prestige, knowledge) as the cause of family violence. Goode argues that the fewer other resources a husband can command, the more likely he is to resort to violence in order to maintain superiority over other family members, especially those who traditionally occupy lower status, such as his wife. Resource theory is a provocative explanation for domestic violence, but it is not a program theory since it does not prescribe any actions for intervention.

In contrast, despite an obvious lack of sophistication, a theory that proposed immediate solutions to prevent spousal abuse, such as stress reduction or avoidance techniques, would qualify as a program theory. Such a theory might be simplistic in assuming that a husband's lack of skills in handling stress causes him to beat his wife, but the theory would be action-oriented, or prescriptive in nature, specifying what actions should be taken to alleviate the problem. Similarly, if Goode (1971) had prescribed the strategy of offering abusive husbands more resources, unlikely as this sounds, then resource theory would have also been a program theory.

Conceptualization of Treatment Format and Implementation Strategy. Since program theory is action-oriented, how such actions are organized becomes an integral concern of program theory. The action part of program theory involves such issues as how the treatment is constructed and implemented, and the conceptualization of these strategies is also prescriptive. A treatment can be designed in different formats in terms of components and strengths. Program theory specifies how the treatment should be constructed for purposes of intervention. Similarly, a given treatment may be implemented in many different ways in terms of types of implementors, modes of delivery, and so on. Assumptions made by program designers regarding the implementation processes are another focus of program theory.

Range of Options in Choosing Outcome Criteria. The selection of which outcome criteria are to be used in an evaluation is a value-laden decision that also reflects the prescriptive aspect of program theory. Different stakeholders have different interests and values regarding a program and, depending on their frames of reference, may also have different preferences and concerns about which outcome criteria should be investigated for evaluation purposes. Due to resource constraints, an evaluation cannot possibly investigate all potential outcome criteria. Those outcome criteria finally selected, therefore, will be only a limited set of a larger pool of potential outcomes that might be affected by the program. The problem is that different outcome criteria influence different evaluation results. Program administrators, for example, may choose criteria related to the maintenance function of an evaluation, while funding agencies may be more interested in criteria related to output performance. These preferences, however, may conflict. A program judged highly on maintenance goals may not necessarily be judged highly on output goals, and vice versa. Program theory must beware of these differences in values and priorities.

Given these three value-oriented aspects of program theory, one must conclude that program theory is concerned not only with causality but also with reform, and that the nature of program theory is prescriptive as well as descriptive. Its dual nature enables program theory to fit John Dewey's (1929, 1933) vision of integrating social sciences with social practice. Dewey opposed the tendency of social scientists to mimic natural scientists in separating theory from practice, arguing that such separation of "science" from "practical application," when applied to social phenomena, prevented social scientists from considering solutions to social problems. Dewey called for the creation of theory that was not only scientifically sound but also relevant to social improvement.

In view of program theory's synthesis of descriptive (or scientific) and prescriptive (or practical) concerns, a new definition of program theory is in order. Program theory is defined here as *a specification of what must be done to achieve desired goals, what other important impacts may also be antici-*

pated, and how these goals and impacts are to be generated. This definition reflects the dual nature of program theory. The first part of the definition is prescriptive, focusing on what the structure and activities of a program should be, including such things as treatments, outcomes, and implementation processes related to the values of the program. The remainder of the definition is oriented toward descriptive theory, dealing with what actually are the underlying mechanisms linking causal relationships among program treatments, implementations, processes, and outcomes.

Program theory can also be categorized into two subtheories. The prescriptive aspect of program theory can be referred to as "normative theory." Normative theory provides guidance on what goals or outcomes should be pursued or examined, and how the treatment should be designed and implemented. The explanatory aspect of program theory can be referred to as "causative theory." Causative theory specifies how a program works by identifying the conditions under which certain processes will arise and what their likely consequences will be.

Normative theory can evolve from unexamined premises, assumptions, customary procedures, and prior theory and knowledge. Because these sources are often taken for granted by program designers or other stakeholders, they are rarely stated or examined, either explicitly or systematically. Nevertheless, normative theory guides program planning, formulation, and implementation, providing the rationale and justification for program structure and activities.

Causative theory, on the other hand, is based on empirical examination of the causal relationship between treatment and outcome. Specifically, causative theory attempts to answer the following questions: How does the treatment affect the outcome? What kinds of intervening factors might mediate the effect of the treatment on the outcome variable? Under which contextual conditions would the causal relationship be facilitated or inhibited?

Approaches to Program Theory Construction

Evaluators have often disagreed on how to construct program theory. While some evaluators, such as Wholey (1987) and Patton (1989), emphasize the viewpoints of program stakeholders, others, such as Chen and Rossi (1980, 1983), contend that program theory should stress social science theory and knowledge. The following discussion contrasts these two approaches and then attempts to reconcile them.

Stakeholder Approach. The stakeholder approach to program theory construction strives to respond to stakeholders' perspectives, ideas, and expectations because the stakeholders sponsor the evaluations and utilize evaluation results. Program theory, therefore, is relevant only insofar as it reflects the stakeholders' values. Wholey and his associates (for example,

Wholey, 1979, 1987; Rutman, 1980) originally developed and applied this approach; Patton (1980, 1989), Trochim (1985, 1989), and McClintock (this volume) have contributed to it.

Wholey and his associates (for example, Wholey, 1979) have stressed the construction of program theory as a key element in evaluability assessment, that is, assessment of the feasibility for evaluating a program in order to upgrade performance. Wholey and his associates have argued that in constructing program theory for the stakeholder approach, evaluators must obtain clues to stakeholder perceptions from both relevant documents and interviews with multiple stakeholders. Relevant documentation includes the program's legislative history, regulations and guidelines, budget justifications, monitoring reports, and reports of program accomplishments. Key policymakers, managers, and interest groups should be questioned regarding their assumptions and expectations about the relationships among program resources, program activities, and expected outcomes. These interviews and site visits should reveal program priorities, expected program accomplishments, relationships between objectives, problems and difficulties facing the program, and information needs.

Evaluators can use their documentation review and interviews to construct a tentative model, which they could then discuss with key stakeholders to highlight the difference in expectations discussed above. This process should facilitate agreements on the intended program theory in terms of program resources, activities, intended outcomes, important side effects, and assumed causal links among resources, activities, and outcomes. After the differences are resolved, a formal program theory can be completed.

Wholey (1987) stresses that the chief purpose of program theory construction is to clarify and develop the key stakeholders' perspectives underlying the program. He urges evaluators to avoid relying on their own knowledge or expertise in constructing program theory, arguing that theory should emerge from the data rather than from prior structures or hypotheses.

Social Science Approach. Chen and Rossi (1980, 1983), on the other hand, advocate a social science approach to program theory. They propose that evaluators derive program theory from the existing body of knowledge as well as from direct observations of program operation, warning evaluators against uncritical acceptance of stakeholders' viewpoints. Chen and Rossi maintain that the reality of the program may not reflect stakeholders' positions. Vested interests may cause stakeholders to stress desirability over the plausibility of the program. A version of theory that appeals to stakeholders in the short run by accentuating desirability may not necessarily be the best for providing insightful understanding of the program in the long run.

Key stakeholders, moreover, tend to base their perceptions of both social problems and program theory on hunch or common sense. A program theory based entirely on stakeholders' perspectives, therefore, might fail to grasp complicated causal processes underlying the program. Evaluators who accepted the stakeholders' positions without question would then be off the mark. For example, official goals are not always operative goals (Perrow, 1961). An evaluator who relied mainly on stakeholders' views in specifying outcomes might dwell on official goals that would not be seriously pursued by the staff. So too, those areas most likely to be affected by operative goals may not be included in the evaluation at all.

Unlike Wholey (1987), Chen and Rossi (1980, 1983) urge evaluators to utilize their expertise and knowledge in constructing program theory, maintaining that program theory based on knowledge of how the program is executed, as well as on social science theory, may facilitate better understanding of program structure, processes, and consequences. Chen and Rossi do not object to the inclusion of key stakeholders' views in formulating program theory; in fact, they advocate including theories constructed from both perspectives in the evaluation, but they have not yet provided detailed procedures or guidelines for synthesizing them.

Integrative Approaches. Each of the approaches to program theory discussed above has its strengths, but an integrative approach that can synthesize them might be even stronger. The stakeholder approach facilitates clarification and development of stakeholders' views, while the social science approach expands program theory by connecting it to social theory. Utilization studies (for example, Weiss and Bucuvales, 1980) suggest that stakeholders may actually need both perspectives. Key stakeholders do not merely expect the evaluation to incorporate their points of view; they also hope the evaluation can provide them with new information and offer them fresh insights about the program.

Evaluators, therefore, need to create integrative models that synthesize the stakeholder and social science approaches. These approaches will require dual theorizing processes. On the one hand, evaluators will have to use the stakeholder approach to clarify and refine key stakeholder perspectives through interviews and documentation review, as described in the previous section. On the other hand, they will need to use the social science approach to construct an alternative program theory based on their knowledge, expertise, and observations of the program. Alternative and often multiple program theories may be generated through the theorizing process.

There are at least two strategies evaluators can use in synthesizing these multiple theories generated from the dual theorizing processes into a final version of program theory. In the first strategy, evaluators use their own professional judgment to refine and develop the final version of program theory, covering issues of concern to both stakeholders and evaluators within time and resource constraints. Bickman and Peterson (this volume) and Riggin (this volume) offer some applications of this version of integrative approaches in finalizing program theory.

Alternatively, a more elaborate integrative approach can be applied to involve key stakeholders in the finalization of program theory. If these stakeholders are available for collaboration, the evaluator can solicit their input to determine which theories or which part of a theory should be included or excluded in the final form of program theory, again within the limits of available resources and time.

The evaluator and key stakeholders will need to review and discuss the implications of these theories in terms of the following issues: What are the strengths and weaknesses of each theory? What kind(s) of information will the theories provide? How will the information relate to policy decision-making processes? The evaluator may then negotiate with the stakeholders to select a version of program theory that best meets the needs of both parties. After reaching some agreement, they can then proceed with the evaluation. This version of the integrative approach may further ensure that stakeholders' perspectives are well incorporated into the program theory for evaluation.

In some cases, the key stakeholders and evaluators may agree during the discussion and negotiation process to focus the final version of theory on either the stakeholder or social science approach. As long as this decision is made through mutual understanding and agreement rather than through arbitrary choices by one party, the validity of the integrative approach will not be challenged. The mutual understanding and consensus will still facilitate utilization of the evaluation results.

Typology of Theory-Driven Evaluations

The framework of program theory discussed above suggests six basic types of theory-driven evaluations (Chen, 1990). As indicated in Figure 1, three types relate to normative theory: normative treatment, normative implementation environment, and normative outcome. The other three pertain to causative theory: impact, intervening mechanism, and generalization. These six basic types of theory-driven evaluations can be briefly defined as follows:

1. *Normative treatment evaluation* identifies the normative structure of the treatment, examines the actual treatment delivered in the field, and assesses the congruence between the normative and implemented treatments.
2. *Normative implementation environment evaluation* identifies the normative implementation environment, examines the actual environment in which the program is implemented, and assesses the congruence between the normative and actual implementation environments.

Figure 1. Program Theory and Evaluation Types

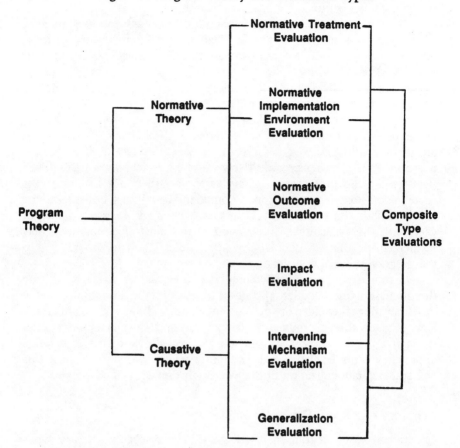

3. *Normative outcome evaluation* seeks to identify the set of normative goals or outcomes to be pursued or examined by the program. This type of evaluation also ascertains whether the resources and program activities are oriented toward these goals or outcomes for facilitating program planning and management.
4. *Impact evaluation* examines a broad base of evidence to assess treatment impact in terms of both plausible intended and unintended outcomes.
5. *Intervening mechanism evaluation* examines the underlying processes mediating between treatment and outcome.
6. *Generalization evaluation* considers how to extend the immediate evaluation results to future situations of interest to the stakeholders.

Two or more of these six basic types may be combined to generate a variety of composite types of theory-driven evaluations (Chen, 1990). For instance, a normative implementation environment evaluation could be combined with an impact evaluation to ease the transition between planning and implementation.

Analytical Techniques for Designing Theory-Driven Evaluations

The design and execution of theory-driven evaluations can benefit from a variety of research methods or techniques. The following discussion examines some of the techniques particularly useful either for normative evaluations or for causative evaluations.

Normative Evaluations. The application of normative evaluations requires assessment of the normative and implemented program structures such as treatment, implementation environment, or outcome. Patterns of normative and implemented program structures can be obtained from interviewing or surveying stakeholders, observing program operations, reviewing the relevant documents or literature, and so on. Research techniques, qualitative or quantitative, that detect, discover, clarify, or develop the normative and implemented patterns of program structures are particularly useful in this area.

If there are a large number of stakeholders' views or opinions that need to be considered, data reduction techniques such as factor analysis, cluster analysis, or multidimensional scaling can be applied to detect the major dimensions of stakeholders' views on the normative program structure. If there are strong disagreements among stakeholders on program structure and if there is a need for evaluators to develop some acceptable version of the normative program structure, evaluators can apply consensus generation methods such as Multi-Attribute Utility Theory, Delphi techniques, and nominal groups to generate some agreements.

In addition, there are useful analytical techniques to measure program structure or guide data collection and data analysis. Scales such as the Multiphasic Environmental Assessment Procedure developed by Moos and associates (for example, Moos, 1988) provide effective measurement of the normative implementation environment. Wholey (1987) indicates that the PERT chart is particularly useful to link resource inputs through a chain of events to final objectives. Marquart (this volume) demonstrates how useful pattern matching can be in developing key stakeholders' views on program treatment, activities, and outcomes as well as in assessing the congruence among stakeholders' views.

Causative Evaluations. Causative evaluations assess the causal processes underlying a program. Analytical strategies such as patch-up designs and pattern matching are particularly useful to broaden the evidence base for impact evaluation. Patch-up designs, according to Cordray (1986), cut across the traditional distinctions of quasi-experimental designs by using whatever procedures are necessary or available to devise a reasonable test of the causal hypothesis. Similarly, Trochim (1989) also argues that pattern matching can enhance the internal validity of an impact evaluation by systematic use of elaborate theoretical patterns of impacts across different programs, participants, or measures. Mark (this volume) proposes additional techniques such as conceptual replication and reversed treatment designs.

Chen and Rossi (1983) argue that structural equation models are useful in analyzing the linkages between the treatment and the outcome in the intervening mechanism evaluation. In addition, Lipsey and Pollard (1989) propose, among others, stage-state models as an alternative strategy to express intervening processes. In the stage-state models, the format of the theory is the transition of persons from one stage or state to another stage or state, such as getting healthier, more knowledgeable, or more employable. Conrad and Buelow (this volume) and Smith (this volume) have designed applications of structural equation modeling to develop and test program theory.

Generalization evaluation concerns the relevance of the evaluation results to future applications. Useful analytical strategies in this area are exemplified by the UTOS scheme in Cronbach (1982) and by implicit and explicit generalization in Chen and Rossi (1987) and Chen (1990). Goitein (1988) has illustrated applications of the implicit and explicit strategies.

Conclusion

Traditional evaluation perspectives such as the experimental paradigm and naturalistic approaches have made important contributions to program evaluation. Excessive, indiscriminate use of method-oriented perspectives, however, may inappropriately tailor an evaluation to meet a particular research method. The concern of the theory-driven perspective is more comprehensive. Research methods are regarded as one of the integral parts of an evaluation rather than as the central activity (Chen, 1990). The application of theory-driven evaluations starts with the clarification and/ or development of program theory ideally created through joint efforts between stakeholders and evaluators. Based on the nature of program theory defined by the stakeholders and evaluators, a particular type of theory-driven evaluation is selected and constructed. The conceptual framework of the theory-driven evaluation then guides the selection of pertinent research methods for data collection and analysis. The integration of program theory into evaluation processes can enhance communication between stakeholders and evaluators with respect to their views and concerns in designing a useful evaluation.

In addition to greater accommodation of policy needs, in the long run theory-driven evaluations may also benefit social reforms more than method-oriented or theoretical types of evaluations. Lessons learned from evaluation experiences in the last three decades have indicated the difficulty and complexity of designing and implementing social programs or policies. Unless evaluators explicitly formulate the normative and causative theories underlying the programs they evaluate, precious knowledge related to program design and implementation may be never examined systematically. Use of the theory-driven perspective will facilitate the accumulation and development of a systematic and comprehensive body of knowledge on how to improve our society.

References

Bickman, L. "The Functions of Program Theory." In L. Bickman (ed.), *Using Program Theory in Evaluation*. New Directions for Program Evaluation, no. 33. San Francisco: Jossey-Bass, 1987.

Chen, H.-T. *Theory-Driven Evaluations*. Newbury Park, Calif.: Sage, 1990.

Chen, H.-T., and Rossi, P. H. "The Multi-Goal, Theory-Driven Approach to Evaluation: A Model Linking Basic and Applied Social Science." *Social Forces*, 1980, *59*, 106–122.

Chen, H.-T., and Rossi, P. H. "Evaluating with Sense: The Theory-Driven Approach." *Evaluation Review*, 1983, *7*, 283–302.

Chen, H.-T., and Rossi, P. H. "The Theory-Driven Approach to Validity." *Evaluation and Program Planning*, 1987, *10*, 95–103.

Cordray, D. S. "Quasi-Experimental Analysis: A Mixture of Methods and Judgment." In W.M.K. Trochim (ed.), *Advances in Quasi-Experimental Design and Analysis*. New Directions for Program Evaluation, no. 31. San Francisco: Jossey-Bass, 1986.

Cronbach, L. J. *Designing Evaluations of Educational and Social Programs*. San Francisco: Jossey-Bass, 1982.

Dewey, J. *The Quest for Certainty*. New York: Minton, Balch, 1929.

Dewey, J. *How We Think*. (Rev. ed.) Lexington, Mass.: Heath, 1933.

Goitein, B. "Is a New Evaluation Always Necessary?" *Evaluation and Program Planning*, 1988, *11*, 43–49.

Goode, W. J. "Force and Violence in the Family." *Journal of Marriage and Family*, 1971, *33*, 624–636.

Hemple, C. *Aspects of Scientific Explanation*. New York: Free Press, 1965.

Kerlinger, F. N. *Foundations of Behavioral Research*. (3rd ed.) New York: Holt, Rinehart & Winston, 1986.

Lave, C. A., and March, J. G. *An Introduction to Models in the Social Sciences*. New York: Harper & Row, 1975.

Lipsey, M. W. "Theory as Method: Small Theories of Treatments." Paper presented at the National Center for Health Services Research Conference: Strengthening Causal Interpretations of Non-Experimental Data, Tucson, Arizona, 1987.

Lipsey, M. W., and Pollard, J. A. "Driving Toward Theory in Program Evaluation: More Models to Choose from." *Evaluation and Program Planning*, 1989, *12*, 317–328.

Moos, R. H. "Assessing the Program Environment: Implications for Program Evaluation and Design." In K. J. Conrad and C. Roberts-Gray (eds.), *Evaluating Program Environment*. New Directions for Program Evaluation, no. 40. San Francisco: Jossey-Bass, 1988.

Patton, M. Q. *Qualitative Evaluation Methods*. Newbury Park, Calif.: Sage, 1980.

Patton, M. Q. "A Context and Boundaries for Theory-Driven Approach to Validity." *Evaluation and Program Planning*, 1989, *12*, 375–377.

Perrow, C. "The Analysis of Goals in Complex Organizations." *American Sociological Review*, 1961, *26*, 855.

Popper, K. R. *The Logic of Scientific Discovery*. New York: Basic Books, 1959.

Rutman, L. *Planning Useful Evaluation: Evaluability Assessment*. Newbury Park, Calif.: Sage, 1980.

Trochim, W.M.K. "Pattern Matching, Construct Validity, and Conceptualization in Program Evaluation." *Evaluation Review*, 1985, *9* (5), 575–604.

Trochim, W.M.K. "Outcome Pattern Matching and Program Theory." *Evaluation and Program Planning*, 1989, *12*, 355–366.

Weiss, C. H., and Bucuvales, M. J. *Social Science Research and Decision-Making*. New York: Columbus Press, 1980.

Wholey, J. S. *Evaluation: Promise and Performance*. Washington, D.C.: Urban Institute, 1979.

Wholey, J. S. "Evaluability Assessment: Developing Program Theory." In L. Bickman (ed.), *Using Program Theory in Evaluation*. New Directions for Program Evaluation, no. 33. San Francisco: Jossey-Bass, 1987.

Huey-tsyh Chen is an associate professor in the Department of Sociology at the University of Akron, Akron, Ohio. He was a guest editor for a 1989 special issue of Evaluation and Program Planning, *which focused on the theory-driven approach. He is the author of* Theory-Driven Evaluations.

Effective administrators function as applied theorists by developing and using generalizable knowledge about programs related to their responsibilities as managers and leaders in organizational settings.

Administrators as Applied Theorists

Charles McClintock

Thinking theoretically is what good administrators do. The effective administrator is someone who combines day-to-day management of program details with a broad vision of organizational leadership. This combination of skills rests on the ability to relate information about the ongoing and often disconnected flow of everyday events to underlying concepts of program purpose, process, and structure. In addition, successful administrators often take an experimental view of organizational life, regularly using information to formulate hypotheses and questions that are tested and revised against the criteria of conventional wisdom and the unfolding of events.

These aspects of administrative practice describe what is meant by the term *applied theorizing*. In formal usage, theorizing is a purely intellectual activity that is pursued by those in scholarly and scientific fields as a means of establishing general knowledge. Validation of basic theoretical knowledge requires empirical hypothesis testing that is as context free as possible. Applied theorizing uses the logic of science but also validates knowledge against what is contextually and politically sensible. Applied theory can derive from experiential sources such as the uncodified artistry of professional practice or the implicit truths of organizational dynamics and political structures and, ultimately, must be tested against its relevance to those sources. Like basic theory, discovery of regularities in applied knowledge that make it generalizable beyond a specific setting is desirable. In applied theorizing, however, the process of experimenting with ideas is at least as important as the knowledge produced. Creating and testing new

I thank Melvin Mark, Jules Marquart, Leslie Riggin, and Carol Wilburn for their thoughtful suggestions about this chapter.

 19

concepts that underlie the dynamics of organizational life infuses programs with energy and makes risk taking and failure acceptable. Indeed, the failure of an experiment often is greater motivation for renewed creativity than is success (Bennis, 1989).

These differences between basic and applied theorizing may only be matters of degree. Theorizing in general is a process that moves back and forth between the abstract and the observable, revises what was taken for granted, includes what was overlooked, complicates with unexpected findings, and simplifies with new interpretations. Understanding more about this process will lead to more effective education of professionals of all kinds who must contend with the complexity, uncertainty, instability, uniqueness, and value conflict that are characteristic of many settings of professional practice (Schön, 1983).

To be most effective, those who assist administrators in developing and improving organizations, such as program evaluators, organizational development consultants, and human resource managers, should orient their work toward the task of applied theorizing. In this chapter a conceptual framework is presented that describes the process of applied theorizing based on how administrators use information to accomplish their managerial and leadership goals. The framework consists of a set of activities and quality criteria that administrators can use as they apply knowledge to guide action and seek knowledge from action. By implication, those who support administrators could use the framework in their work to create studies, reports, and other informational products based on a shared perspective of how knowledge guides and derives from action in organizational settings.

Overall, the perspective on administrative behavior presented here was developed from several organizational case studies. While the framework is empirically based it also reflects the values and assumptions of organizational learning (Argyris and Schön, 1978). Theorizing as learning involves an ongoing dialogue between assumptions and expectations and the evidence that is gathered to examine their realization. The terms "successful" and "effective" reflect a blend of empirical grounding (that is, certain behaviors were correlated with individuals who were identified by others as successful) and researcher values that guide attention to behavioral correlates of success related to theorizing. Alternative perspectives might focus on other behaviors, for example, power seeking, entrepreneurship, or defensiveness, which would imply different criteria for success or effectiveness.

Program Theory and Administrative Behavior

A critical part of applied theorizing consists of knowledge of the organization's production or service delivery process, such as how to manufacture a better computer, how to cure a patient's medical condition, or how to educate a socially and ethnically diverse population of students. Especially in service organizations, this knowledge often is based on implicit models of causal processes that are not well understood (McClintock, 1987b). Also, while related to basic scientific concepts, these models often rely on uncodified experiential knowledge that makes it difficult to share and apply professional wisdom in a particular situation (Schön, 1983). Note that this causal knowledge is a part of all professional practice that involves intentional interventions in order to achieve some desired outcome (House, Mathison, and McTaggart, 1989). For example, a social worker provides family counseling where child abuse has occurred, a teacher develops a tutoring program for underachieving students, an employer offers a child care program to employees to boost their productivity and reduce absenteeism, and a doctor performs a battery of tests in search of the cause and treatment for an acutely ill patient. In each case these complex professional judgments contain "theories" of causality (often implicit and difficult to articulate), in which certain factors are thought to produce undesirable effects, thus implying interventions designed to change or counteract the negative causes. As applied organizational theorists, administrators should be conversant with this knowledge even though they may not use it directly in their work.

A second set of issues concerns the organizational aspects of implementing these models (Scheirer, 1987). Thus, administrators must be able to address perennial problems such as lack of sufficient funding for departments to achieve their goals, employee communications and morale that are in crisis, and specialization and compartmentalization of professional staff that inhibit creative collaboration. These examples point to the need for administrators to be able to apply knowledge about concepts such as finance and budgeting, decision making and motivation, and professionalization and organizational structure in order to ensure the success of their basic programs.

Finally, it may not always be clear what program outcomes should be included in a model that can be used to evaluate effectiveness or goal attainment. Generally, this issue involves defining values or criteria that are used to judge whether outcomes are useful or valid. Given the three aforementioned examples of manufacturing, health care, and education, administrators struggle to balance competing values for outcomes such as short-term versus long-term profitability, quality versus efficiency of care, and minimum competence versus excellence.

As described in other chapters in this volume (see Chen or Riggin), this knowledge—causal models of a program's production or service delivery process, implementation issues, and outcomes or criteria used to evaluate effectiveness—is what is included in the term "program theory." The concept of administrative theorizing expands on this formulation of program theory to describe how administrators use information about causality, implementation, and valued outcomes in service of their roles as managers and leaders.

Every administrator confronts a daily stream of puzzles and problems, most of which are not structured for easy analysis and solution. Administrative work is fragmented into diverse, short episodes of information exchange (Mintzberg, 1973). It is difficult to exchange wisdom and easy to feel buried in detail unless one can consolidate the high volume of seemingly disparate information in order to identify those underlying factors of program production and implementation that will produce desired outcomes for different groups.

Given this context, thinking theoretically is crucial to administrative success. It is estimated that organizations spend billions of dollars a year in administrators' time reinventing program theories when individuals move into a new organization or encounter unfamiliar issues (Dutton and Starbuck, 1963). This inefficiency is largely due to the absence of a language that administrators and their staff can use to describe the specific programs and issues in generic conceptual terms. Thus, program theory and the process of applied theorizing have enormous value as ways of framing issues so that they can be generalized across organizational settings and subject matter.

An example of administrative behavior that illustrates the advantage of thinking theoretically about programs is shown in the following episode: An educational administrator was confronted with competing information from a faculty curriculum committee, a student group, and a classroom-scheduling office regarding a proposal to increase the number of midterm exams. The proposal was loosely based on a theory of educating in which it was implicitly hypothesized that increases in the frequency of performance feedback would lead to greater understanding and retention of content. Once this two-variable hypothesis was made explicit, the administrator worked with each group to develop a more complex theory involving additional factors that might moderate the relationship between testing and learning, such as the type of course (introductory versus advanced seminar) and the methods of testing knowledge (in-class exam versus take-home essay). Additional outcomes such as self-directed learning also were identified that, together with the moderating factors, began to define a theory of classroom instruction that was grounded in the realities of a particular educational organization. Discussing the proposal in terms of additional cause-and-effect concepts added uncertainty to each group's perspective. The increased uncertainty, however, made it easier to view the policy change as an experiment and to focus on how it should be implemented and evaluated. Framing the proposal in this manner also minimized aimless conversation and confrontational communication since discussion focused on testing a model of learning and not on whether some particular proposal won or lost. In addition, the instructional theory served as a form of institutional memory by creating a framework for periodic evaluation of the policy and for discussion of related issues such as the design of instructional support programs and evaluation of teaching.

This example illustrates how it is possible to link different ideas into an applied theoretical framework that can focus discussion, guide action and information gathering, identify connections among policies and programs, and facilitate generalization of knowledge across time and setting. Thus, applied theorizing is a way of organizing knowledge to guide action and of acquiring knowledge from action.

Methods of Applied Theorizing

What distinguishes applied theorizing from a general process of conceptualization is that it is linked to action with the goal of improving programs and policies—a process sometimes referred to as formative evaluation (McClintock, 1986). The concepts of program theory and formative evaluation provide a link between administrative behavior and applied theorizing. While administrators work with many aspects of organizations, including power, resources, structural arrangements, and people, the common medium or "technology" of their work is information. Administrators can be thought of as information brokers whose vested interest is program improvement (McClintock, 1987b). Improvement of programs requires ongoing formative evaluation that focuses on two aspects of program theory: (1) action or performance issues such as describing client needs, allocating resources, supervising staff effort, monitoring program activities, and documenting results and (2) conceptual or structural issues such as identifying underlying models of program production and implementation, reframing problems and solutions, organizing programs and roles, and clarifying strategic values and goals (McClintock, 1986, 1987a).

While there are formal analytical methods for addressing these aspects of programs, it is difficult, based on the research literature alone, to describe the more informal day-to-day activities that administrators might pursue. Thus, it is necessary to fall back on terms such as professional artistry and wisdom to describe how effective administrators use information to understand program theory and establish a process of applied theorizing. To fill this gap, I designed five case studies—consisting of a for-profit aerospace company, a not-for-profit university, a health care service, a professional association, and a public-sector agency of state government—to describe administrators' informal or tacit knowledge about using information to improve programs. Data were collected in several waves of interviews and observations of administrators and others in the case study organizations. The units of analysis were not people or organizations but rather behaviors and processes related to information brokering and program improvement (McClintock, 1985). Questions and observations were derived from overlapping perspectives on administrative behavior, including the concepts of reflective practice (Schön, 1983), practical intelligence (Wagner and Sternberg, 1985), organizational learning (Argyris and Schön, 1978), and implicit theories of causality (Salancik and Porac, 1986). Exhibit 1 contains a list of administrative activities related to information management that were developed from the literature and reported with regularity in the case studies. This list conveys a sense of the pluralism and fragmentation that characterize the information environment of administrative work and describes the challenge of strategic thinking and action related to critical program processes. The activities in Exhibit 1 can be thought of as methods or tools of applied theorizing, but they require a focus on issues if they are to illuminate the underlying purposes, processes, and structures of program functioning. Without this connection to larger issues, these administrative activities become ends in themselves, similar to method-driven research in search of a theory or conceptual framework.

Administrative Strategies for Applied Theorizing

While most administrators examined in the case studies were skilled at several of the activities in Exhibit 1, several individuals were able to con-

Exhibit 1. Administrative Activities Related to Information Management

Synthesize ideas from different groups
Increase complexity/uncertainty with new information about valued outcomes
Clarify implicit theories of program production or implementation
Link individual and program goals
Write plans for achieving short-term goals
Make connections between people with related interests
Define mission and long-term goals
Create vision and symbolize overlapping values
Mediate and manage conflict
Identify unmet needs and required actions for correction
Propose models and frameworks for action
Train and develop staff around concepts that underlie program activity
Reduce complexity and uncertainty with focus on single options
Produce procedure and policy manuals, decision processes, and agendas
Establish priorities and incentives
Present a rationale or analogy for choice or action
Connect specific activities to broader purposes and values
Create support for program plans and project proposals
Discover external influences on programs
Search and analyze various information sources
Make comparisons among programs and over time
Convene meetings, committees, and groups
Identify critical success factors
Provide feedback on performance of programs and individuals
Commission studies and reviews
Collect and distribute data
Defend accountability in terms of basic program values and purposes

solidate and relate them to broader administrative strategies of using information for program improvement. The categories described below emerged from the literature and the case study data as summaries of administrative strategies for applied theorizing. They are collections of methods for directly working with the components of program theory—causal models, implementation issues, and valued outcomes—and constitute the purposes and processes of using theory in action. Because of the emphasis on using information, the categories constitute a common framework for reports and communications that could be used by administrators, staff, and consultants. This framework moves beyond the knowledge embodied in program theory to the application of knowledge in professional practice. Both knowledge and how it is used are essential to applied theorizing.

These strategies for applied theorizing are defined in terms of two broad dimensions of administrative work: management and leadership. As managers, administrators are expected to know the details of program functioning and often are faced with complex tasks of processing and communicating vast amounts of information that are integral to program operations. A manager is supposed to be action-oriented and have a hands-on knowledge of how programs are performing (Boyatzis, 1985).

As leaders, administrators are expected to see the forest more than the trees, to convey strategic program vision, and to think conceptually about underlying program structure (Bennis, 1989). Successful administrators have been described as individuals who are able to identify the critical underlying factors amidst a sea of informational detail that will result in achieving program goals or preventing program failure (Rockhart, 1979; Cameron, 1984). Both of these responsibilities require a capacity for applied theorizing: in the former case to reduce the volume and complexity of information to manageable chunks, and in the latter to conceptualize disparate and often conflicting stakeholder agendas in frameworks that make them more compatible.

Managerial Strategies.

Exchanging and Coordinating. As managers, administrators are faced with the fragmentation, redundancy, and information overload of organizational life. Their task is to find ways of exchanging information, coordinating individuals with related interests and connecting people and ideas in order to stimulate action. Many of these activities are associated with directing paper flow, hence the ubiquitous FYI (For Your Information) sign that indicates the presence of an administrative hand. Exchange and coordination is also an interpersonal process aimed at creating behavioral and cognitive connections among people and is implemented through meetings and social occasions of various kinds. Administrators often use exchange and coordination as a way of mediating conflict or resisting proposals that they believe would create unnecessary barriers. To some extent these administrative activities increase uncertainty for others since they add new, unfamiliar information or disrupt existing ways of thinking and acting. To be effective as a strategy for applied theorizing, the ultimate purpose of exchange and coordination must be to identify underlying concepts and commitments that will guide individual and collective action.

Deciding and Acting. Notwithstanding prescriptive models of decision making in which many alternatives are carefully evaluated prior to choice, the social psychological basis of action and decision often requires that options be narrowed or simplified, and attention directed to a single alternative (Brunnson, 1982). Speculative consideration of many options can paralyze action and create decisions by the avoidance of choice (Cohen, March, and Olsen, 1972). In the case studies administrators made use of standard operating procedures, goals, constraints, and regular reminders as ways of narrowing alternatives and stimulating decision and action. The dynamic of the decision and action strategy is to focus attention, sometimes to only one alternative, but to do so in a spirit of experimentation where action is viewed as the operational definition of a hypothesis that can be revised.

Monitoring and Evaluating. Administrators are expected to account for organizational resources and identify the resulting programmatic efforts and outcomes. This is a very difficult task since resources are usually not allocated in terms of program objectives, implementation easily diverges from plans, and there is often disagreement about what outcomes to measure or how to operationally define them. Administrators in the case studies monitored and evaluated programs by discovering external influences, searching data bases and opinion sources, making comparisons among and within programs over time, identifying critical success factors, providing feedback on programs and persons, commissioning studies, and distributing data and reports. Most administrators distinguished between the monitoring and evaluation related to improvement of internal program operations and the information needed for external reporting and accountability. The most effective administrators sought to link these two purposes in order to clarify program models, identify implementation barriers and interdependencies among groups, and reinforce important values and objectives.

Leadership Strategies. Leadership can be thought of as the management of meaning. As leaders, administrators are expected to educate, inspire, and symbolize (Bennis, 1989). These responsibilities require using information with an eye toward its broader and deeper effects on the culture of the organization, recognizing that the meaning of information will vary as it is constructed by different individuals and groups. Leviton and Hughes (1981) describe how program-related information can have different effects to be interpreted for various purposes. Specifically, they identify three uses of the results of program evaluation: (1) conceptual use in which information results in new ways of defining problems and solutions, (2) instrumental use that focuses on means-ends connections, and (3) symbolic use in which information helps persuade people. These ways of using information are similar to the behavior of administrators in the case studies in terms of the following strategies for using information as leaders.

Educating. By virtue of their position in the organization, it is administrators more than anyone else who experience the loosely coupled marketplace of events and perceptions that constitutes life in organizations. Administrators are challenged to relate this heterogeneous environment to underlying forces and purposes that will produce program excellence, without at the same time scattering their own energy in too many directions. Administrators in the case studies did this by conceptualizing models of program causality, reframing problems and solutions, focusing others' attention on unnoticed risks and opportunities, and identifying the interdependencies among activities and groups in the program that were critical to success.

Motivating. In terms of program management and implementation, the two largest areas of responsibility are budget-based planning and personnel. Many administrators in the case studies had difficulty linking these two activities, which reflects a broader historical separation between line-item and program budgeting on the one hand and program and personnel evaluation on the other. A few administrators sought connections between their responsibilities in planning and budgeting and the time-consuming challenges of managing personnel issues. Motivation was the linking concept, making connections between people and plans, identifying structural incentives for individual behavior, and providing information to others that helped them manage their own success. Each of these activities had a practical means-ends orientation, such as program development or improvement of productivity through efficiency of effort or increasing quality. The emphasis was on finding common ground for the actions of different groups, and on short-term planning in the context of long-term goals.

Persuading. Administrators are often called upon to persuade others through the symbolic activities of defining mission and vision. To say that administrators make use of symbolism is not to label them as unusually manipulative. They are as much a part of a social and organizational culture as anyone else and, indeed, are expected to symbolically embody this culture through the use of language, anecdotes, and values. For example, academic administrators who are scholars, aerospace administrators who are engineers, or health administrators who are doctors are likely to be more persuasive leaders than are those who cannot symbolize in action the core values of their organizations. Administrators in the case studies used information to persuade by identifying underlying principles and goals, conducting studies and reviews that were perceived as open and fair, and distributing information and reports based on credible methodologies.

To summarize, administrative methods for applied theorizing can be arrayed across three managerial strategies (exchanging/coordinating, deciding/acting, and monitoring/evaluating) and three leadership strategies (educating, motivating, and persuading). These six strategies for applied theorizing describe how administrators use information to improve programs by influencing underlying program dynamics and establishing knowledge that is generalizable across people and settings.

Management and leadership strategies are separable conceptually but their particular methods are intertwined. Table 1 classifies the various activities of Exhibit 1 in terms of the overlapping dimensions of management and leadership. This framework illustrates the connection between specific administrative activities and broader strategies of applied theorizing.

Judging the Quality of Applied Theorizing

Given this view of administrative behavior, how might one judge the quality of an administrator as an applied theorist? Similarly, how can staff and outside consultants who conduct studies and prepare reports for administrators pursue their work in ways that facilitate applied theorizing? The answers to these questions center on two interrelated approaches to epistemology: scientific and substantive criteria for generating knowledge (Schön, 1983; Weick, 1989).

Administrators can and do act like scientists despite the fact that applied theorizing usually is not based on formal research studies. In the case studies administrators often were sensitive to the kinds of shortcomings of scientific inference that can characterize intuitive social judgment (Nisbett and Ross, 1980). For example, in responding to a crisis they were careful to stratify their opinion gathering across groups with different views and objectives in order to avoid overgeneralizing from small but vivid sample incidents. Schön (1983, pp. 236–266) describes examples of reflective administrative behavior that rely on the logic of experimental hypothesis testing and internal validity for assessing causality. Several administrators in the case studies were able to look at their programs as theories that deserved study, and they made use of comparison groups or time periods as a way of assessing alternative explanations for observable outcomes. Others also made use of the rules of construct validity for adequate measurement of concepts and the rules of external validity for assessing generalizability of propositions. For example, many administrators invoked the logic of interrater reliability by obtaining independent assessments as a means of taking a more consistent measure of a situation, and cluster sampling by carefully selecting advisers who could reflect the heterogeneity of opinion among stakeholders.

Researchers may underestimate these skills and risk misplaced confidence in the rigor of formal research studies in comparison with administrative theorizing. For instance, the following quotation from a leading text on program evaluation methods sells short the scientific abilities of many

Table 1. Administrator Strategies and Methods for Applied Theorizing

	Leadership Strategies		
	Educating	*Motivating*	*Persuading*
Management Strategies			
Exchanging/ Coordinating	Synthesize ideas from different groups	Link individual and program goals	Define mission and long-term goals
	Increase complexity and uncertainty with new information about valued outcomes	Write plans for achieving short-term goals	Create vision and symbolize overlapping values
	Clarify implicit theories of program production or implementation	Make connections between people with related interests	Mediate and manage conflict
	1	2	3
Deciding/ Acting	Identify unmet needs and required actions for correction	Reduce complexity and uncertainty with focus on single options	Present a rationale or analogy for choice or action
	Propose models and frameworks as experiments for action	Produce procedure and policy manuals, decision processes, and agendas	Connect specific activities to broader purposes and values
	Train and develop staff around concepts that underlie program activity	Establish priorities and incentives	Create support for program plans and project proposals
	4	5	6
Monitoring/ Evaluating	Discover external influences on programs	Convene meetings, committees, and groups	Commission studies and reviews
	Search and analyze various information sources	Identify critical success factors	Collect and distribute data
	Make comparisons among programs and over time	Provide feedback on performance of programs and individuals	Defend accountability in terms of basic program values and purposes
	7	8	9

Source: Adapted from McClintock, 1987b.

administrators and limits the possibilities for collaborative theorizing: "The weakest point of the use of program administrator judgments is that it is too much to expect administrators to apply the appropriate attitude of skepticism toward their work that is necessary for them to make hard judgments. A properly conducted impact assessment takes as its guiding hypothesis that the project has no effects, a stance that runs exactly counter to the principle that should guide the administration of a project, namely, that the intervention does have important effects on participants. To expect ordinary mortals to hold both hypotheses simultaneously is unrealistic. . . . In addition, there is an understandable tendency for administrators to want to put their projects in the best of all possible lights, a motivation that may act to downplay or actively suppress negative information on effectiveness" (Rossi and Freeman, 1985, p. 315).

This quote misses a critical distinction about administrative behavior. Often it is true that administrators portray their programs in unrealistically positive terms, especially for evaluators, journalists, or other outsiders who are in positions of judgment. While administrators in general may not want to expose program shortcomings to the public eye, effective administrators are able to identify failure points and make difficult decisions about correcting them. To do this they are constantly testing the validity of program information against scientific and substantive criteria. Far from simultaneously holding only two contradictory hypotheses, administrators often juggle a dozen or more multivariate hypotheses that represent diverse stakeholder perspectives and competing program theories.

Scientific method is not a sufficient basis, however, to describe how administrators behave like applied theorists. In any profession there are standards of appraisal that derive from the situation or the practitioner's role. Based on the case study data and research literature, Table 2 describes substantive criteria for judging the quality of administrators as applied theorists. Some of these criteria incorporate the logic of scientific method (for example, cells 7 and 9); as a group, however, they consist of the managerial and leadership responsibilities of administrators.

The actions and questions in Tables 1 and 2 can be useful to administrators to clarify the concentrations and gaps in their applied theorizing. For instance, some individuals described themselves in terms of the methods and criteria in cells 2, 5, and 7 of both tables. These were individuals who were likely to be labeled as good managers but poor leaders. They appeared to be sensitive to the underlying models and dynamics of program activity but were not adept at creating or conveying those concepts to others. In contrast, some administrators were successful as leaders in cells, 3, 6, and 9 but were unable to translate their charisma into procedures for organizational learning as described in cells, 1, 4, and 7.

Staff and consultants who work with administrators can also use the methods and the questions in Tables 1 and 2 to orient their analyses and

Table 2. Criteria for Judging the Quality of Applied Theorizing

	Leadership Strategies		
	Educating	*Motivating*	*Persuading*
Management Strategies			
Exchanging/ Coordinating	Are perceptual deadlocks broken?	Are most people attached to one or more short-term goals?	Can most people identify the mission of the program or organization?
	Are new concepts, theories, problems, questions, or values discovered?	Are problems or issues discovered that allow existing solutions to be pursued?	Is it possible to explain diverse or conflicting decisions in terms of underlying principles, values, or goals?
	Is new thinking generated about causes of a problem or the possible effects of different solutions?	Are new connections made among people with related interests?	
	1	2	3
Deciding/ Acting	Are costs, risks, benefits, or opportunities identified or redefined?	Does information help motivate staff, clients, or others to act or reach a decision?	Are people with diverse interests and values persuaded to provide political or financial support?
	Are training and development used to convey a conceptual understanding of the work?	Does information clarify specific means-ends connections or selectively reinforce a desired behavior?	Is it possible to resist a request for action or resources by attaching it to a negative principle, value, or goal?
	Are decisions and actions viewed as hypotheses that are subject to revision from experience?		
	4	5	6
Monitoring/ Evaluating	Are external influences, behavior patterns, explanations, or moderating factors discovered?	Is information detailed, timely, and relevant to an underlying model for action?	Is information defensible as systematic, trustworthy, or scientific?
	Is there new understanding of how one activity or group influences or relates to other activities or groups?	Does information help people monitor their own activities in terms of program processes and goals?	Does information appear to diverse audiences as plausible or rational?
	7	8	9

Source: Adapted from McClintock, 1987b.

reports to the gaps or weaknesses in applied theorizing for a particular setting. For programs that are handicapped by conflict or poor communication, cells 1, 2, and 3 could be used to guide formative inquiry for program improvement. Alternatively, a common problem in organizations is that there is too much information and too many untested alternatives for action. In this situation strategies of evaluation and analysis might focus most effectively on cells, 4, 5, and 6.

Conclusion

Successful administrators have been described as those who can think theoretically about their programs. A framework was presented for describing the process of applied theorizing as practiced by effective administrators, which by implication could also be used by consultants and staff who work with administrators. Theorizing refers to the process of identifying abstract constructs distilled from observable details of reality, and of specifying a variety of relationships among them that characterize their taxonomic, systemic, or causal structures. Applied theorizing involves doing these things with an eye toward the application of the constructs in the world of professional practice and organizational behavior.

Applied theorizing is valuable because it is an efficient means of coping with the complex information environment of organizations and also because it is an effective way of creating knowledge that can be shared across time and place. Administrators, staff, and consultants are of most value to each other and their organizations when they exchange knowledge, not just information, among themselves. For this reason, it is important to add theoretical thinking to the list of attributes of the well-managed organization.

References

Argyris, C., and Schön, D. A. *Organizational Learning: A Theory of Action Perspective.* Reading, Mass.: Addison-Wesley, 1978.

Bennis, W. *Why Leaders Can't Lead: The Unconscious Conspiracy Continues.* San Francisco: Jossey-Bass, 1989.

Boyatzis, R. E. *The Competent Manager: A Model for Effective Performance.* New York: Wiley, 1985.

Brunnson, M. "The Irrationality of Action and Action Rationality: Decisions, Ideologies, and Organizational Actions." *Journal of Management Studies,* 1982, *19,* 29-44.

Cameron, K. S. "The Effectiveness of Ineffectiveness." *Research in Organizational Behavior,* 1984, *6,* 235-285.

Cohen, M. D., March, J. G., and Olsen, J. P. "A Garbage Can Model of Organizational Choice." *Administrative Science Quarterly,* 1972, *17,* 1-25.

Dutton, J. M., and Starbuck, W. H. "On Managers and Theories." *Management International,* 1963, *6,* 1-11.

House, E. R., Mathison, S., and McTaggart, R. "Validity and Teacher Inference." *Educational Researcher,* Oct. 1989, pp. 11-15.

Leviton, L. C., and Hughes, E. F. "Research on the Utilization of Evaluation: A Review and Synthesis." *Evaluation Review,* 1981, *5,* 525-548.

McClintock, C. "Process Sampling: A Method for Case Study Research on Administrative Behavior." *Educational Administration Quarterly,* 1985, *21,* 205-222.

McClintock, C. "Toward a Theory of Formative Evaluation." In M. W. Lipsey and D. S. Cordray (eds.), *Evaluation Studies Review Annual.* Vol. 11. Newbury Park, Calif.: Sage, 1986.

McClintock, C. "Conceptual and Action Heuristics: Tools for the Evaluator." In L. Bickman (ed.), *Using Program Theory in Evaluation.* New Directions for Program Evaluation, no. 33. San Francisco: Jossey-Bass, 1987a.

McClintock, C. "Administrators as Information Brokers: A Managerial Perspective on Naturalistic Evaluation." *Evaluation and Program Planning,* 1987b, *10,* 315-323.

Mintzberg, H. *The Nature of Managerial Work.* New York: Harper & Row, 1973.

Nisbett, R., and Ross, L. *Human Inference: Strategies and Shortcomings of Social Judgment.* Englewood Cliffs, N.J.: Prentice-Hall, 1980.

Rockhart, J. F. "Chief Executives Define Their Own Data Needs." *Harvard Business Review,* 1979, *57,* 81-93.

Rossi, P. H., and Freeman H. E. *Evaluation: A Systematic Approach.* (3rd ed.) Newbury Park, Calif.: Sage, 1985.

Salancik, G. R., and Porac, J. E. "Distilled Ideologies: Values Derived from Causal Reasoning in Complex Environments." In H. P. Sims, Jr., D. A. Gioia, and Associates (eds.), *The Thinking Organization: Dynamics of Organizational Social Cognition.* San Francisco: Jossey-Bass, 1986.

Scheirer, M. A. "Program Theory and Implementation Theory: Implications for Evaluators." In L. Bickman (ed.), *Using Program Theory in Evaluation.* New Directions for Program Evaluation, no. 33. San Francisco: Jossey-Bass, 1987.

Schön, D. A. *The Reflective Practitioner.* New York: Basic Books, 1983.

Wagner, R. K., and Sternberg, R. J. "Practical Intelligence in Real-World Pursuits: The Role of Tacit Knowledge." *Journal of Personality and Social Psychology,* 1985, *49,* 436-458.

Weick, K. E. "Theory Construction as Disciplined Imagination." *Academy of Management Review,* 1989, *14,* 516-531.

Charles McClintock is an associate dean in the College of Human Ecology and a professor in the Department of Human Service Studies at Cornell University, Ithaca, New York. His teaching and research focus on administrative behavior and program evaluation methods.

PART TWO

Methodological Approaches

The benefits of program theory will not fully accrue unless program theory is tested; alternative approaches to such testing are discussed.

From Program Theory to Tests of Program Theory

Melvin M. Mark

Although it is not a new idea, the notion of employing theory in program evaluation has received increasing attention in recent years (Bickman, 1987b; Chen, 1989; Chen and Rossi, 1980, 1983, 1987; this volume). One question is whether the literature on theory-driven evaluation, to use Chen and Rossi's terminology, or on program theory, to use the terminology preferred by Bickman and others (for example, Trochim, 1989), leaves us with an improved ability to evaluate programs.

Certainly, the literature on theory in evaluation has given us a better sense of the potential benefits of using program theory (Bickman, 1987a; Chen and Rossi, 1980, 1983). Further, there have been advances in methods for developing program theory, either through structured responses of such informants as program personnel (for example, Conrad and Buelow, this volume; Trochim, 1985, 1989), through review of program documentation, interviews and observation (for example, Bickman, 1985; Riggin, this volume), or through application of social science concepts (for example, Chen and Rossi, 1980, 1983).

What has been lacking in the literature on program theory is a well-articulated approach to developing tests of program theory, once a program theory has been constructed. It is conceivable that some benefits of program theory will accrue without testing the theory. For instance,

The author thanks Leonard Bickman for helpful comments on this chapter. Numerous colleagues provided helpful feedback on a larger manuscript from which this is drawn; the conceptual assistance of Chip Reichardt and William Trochim is especially noteworthy and appreciated.

McClintock (this volume) argues that simply constructing a program theory is a useful form of formative evaluation. However, to reap some of the potential benefits of program theory, such as generalizable explanations, guidance to policymakers, and contributions to substantive social science theory, it is not enough to have constructed a program theory; one must also have reasonable confidence that the theory provides a satisfactory account of what really transpires. That is, one needs to test the theory. The present chapter is designed to provide some general guidelines as to the variety of forms that such tests might take.

The Context of This Chapter

Numerous authors have offered definitions of program theory; for a review of several of these, see Chen (this volume). These definitions all point out that a program theory specifies a causal mechanism (Rosenbaum, 1984) or causal process (Mark, 1986). That is, program theories specify "aspects of the various biological, chemical, physical, [psychological,] or social processes by which the treatment produces its effects" (Rosenbaum, 1984, p. 42). In other words, good program theories indicate "the mediational mechanism or causal sequence through which the treatment produces the effect" (Mark, 1986, p. 57).

The present chapter focuses on tests of the causal mechanisms inherent in good program theory and through which programs are thought to achieve their effects. Thus, the focus is on a restricted set of evaluation activities. Indeed, the testing of causal mechanisms is not relevant to all forms of theory-driven evaluations. Rather, such testing seems relevant to the evaluation types that Chen (this volume) classifies under causative theory, but not to those classified under normative theory. Program theories can alternatively be tested, for instance, in terms of their descriptive accuracy in classifying types of local projects (see, for example, Conrad and Buelow, this volume.

Prior Recommendations about Testing Program Theory

The most common suggestion about how to test program theory is to employ some form of causal modeling (Chen and Rossi, 1983, 1987; Costner, 1989; Smith, this volume). While causal modeling (for example, LISREL models, structural equation models) does represent one approach to testing program theory, it is only one approach. Further, causal modeling has limits. Indeed, Chen and Rossi (Chen 1989, p. 303) indicate that their earlier work "may have been overly optimistic with regard to the use of selection bias modeling techniques to insure internal validity."

As alternatives to causal modeling, Cordray (1989) recommends the use of multiple methodologies, including patched-up designs and metanalysis. These recommendations are quite sound, but they do not specify what is unique about testing program theory. That is, these methods can be used equally well for estimating effects in a "black box" evaluation, and the theory-driven evaluator needs to know how to apply these or other methods specifically to test program theory.

Trochim (1989) has recently suggested that program theory can be tested through pattern matching (for an application of Trochim's approach, see Marquart, this volume). Put simply, the idea is that theoretical patterns should be compared with observed patterns, and that a strong match between the two supports the theory. The present chapter offers suggestions that can be readily expressed in a pattern-matching framework. This chapter might even be read as a companion piece to the conceptual component of the Trochim (1985) paper, with the sections that follow offering a variety of suggestions about how to develop more elaborate theoretical patterns to test.

Elaboration or Pattern Matching in Testing Program Theory

It appears that there is one general mechanism, alternatively labeled elaboration (Rosenbaum, 1984) or pattern matching (Campbell, 1966; Trochim, 1985, 1989), that underlies all efforts to test causal mechanisms. Put simply, in elaboration or pattern matching the researcher considers the implications of prospective causal mechanisms in order to generate an elaborate pattern of predictions. The researcher compares the observed pattern with the patterns predicted by the alternative process models; support for a particular process model comes from a good fit between predicted and observed patterns (though as yet no well-developed standards of "good fit" exist for this approach).

Many methodologists and statisticians have recognized the value of having more complex (as opposed to simpler) predicted patterns of results (see, for example, Campbell, 1966, 1975, esp. pp. 182-183; Platt, 1984). In discussing how to draw causal inferences from observational studies (that is, quasi-experiments), Rosenbaum (1984) emphasizes the importance of specifying and testing a pattern of predictions based on the hypothesized causal mechanism. Rosenbaum (1984, p. 43) also cites a number of methodological and statistical experts who have given similar advice. For example, Cochran (1965, p. 252) reports that when asked, "What can be done in observational studies to clarify the step from association to causation, Sir Ronald Fisher replied: 'Make your theories elaborate.'" Subsequent discussion revealed that Fisher meant "when constructing a causal hypothesis one should envisage as many *different* consequences of the truth as possible, and plan observational studies to discover whether each of these consequences is found to hold" (Cochran, 1965, p. 252).

Exhortations to elaborate do not, however, aid the researcher in thinking about how to develop a complex theoretical pattern to test against observed data. The goal of the remaining sections is to suggest alternative ways to elaborate, that is, to suggest forms of hypotheses that are useful in testing program theory. Because testing of theory in evaluation has been relatively rare (Lipsey and others, 1985), many of the examples here are hypothetical or from other research areas.

Mediating Variables as a Form of Elaboration

As noted earlier, the most common suggestion for testing program theory is to conduct some form of causal modeling. Program theory would be used to identify potential mediators or variables through which the treatment has its effect on other outcomes of interest. The hypothesized mediator(s) would be measured, and causal modeling techniques would be applied to test the hypothesized relationship between the treatment, the mediator(s), and the outcomes (Chen and Rossi, 1987; Judd and Kenny, 1981; Smith, this volume; and Mark, 1986, who has labeled causal modeling and other techniques that could be used to observe mediation as "process tracing").

The identification of potential mediators, and the predictions of causal modeling about the interrelations among the treatment, mediators, and outcomes (Judd and Kenny, 1981), can be recognized as a form of elaboration. Program theory leads to a more elaborate set of predictions, in this case involving mediators, than does a black box model of the program.

Despite its many advocates, the causal modeling approach has limitations. Even in its strongest forms, this type of approach to testing program theory is essentially correlational in that the process is simply observed as it occurs. Inferences from this approach can be strengthened, for example, by the careful use of measurement models (Baron and Kenny, 1986). Nevertheless, traditional causal modeling is correlational and open to alternative interpretations.

The criticism of causal modeling focuses on misspecification, which, defined broadly, includes the omission of important variables from the model and the inadequate measurement of variables in the model, and on the failure to meet assumptions; such problems can have severe consequences for estimates. Critiques of causal modeling techniques (for example, Baumrind, 1983; Freedman, 1987) are illuminating and inspire proper caution. Causal modeling techniques can also be criticized, at least with respect to applications to program evaluation, for inadequacies in the theory needed to generate good models (Lipsey and Pollard, 1989).

Of course, causal modeling techniques are not the only method for testing mediation. Simpler procedures can and often have been used, including (1) sequential tests of effects on a process measure and an outcome measure, as is common in social psychology where an analysis of variance or similar device is applied first to a manipulation check (a measure of the hypothesized mediator) and then to an outcome measure (see Lipsey and Pollard, 1989, on the "basic two-step"), (2) demonstration of a correlation between the process measure and the outcome variable, and (3) hierarchical regression or partial correlation (see Brett and James, 1984, for examples). However, like their causal modeling cousins, these techniques are essentially correlational investigations of process and share the same basic shortcomings. Further, these quantitative procedures all have weaknesses relative to their causal modeling alternatives, in terms of clarity of the demonstrated mediation (Baron and Kenny, 1986; Brett and James, 1984; Judd and Kenny, 1981).

Perhaps the bottom line of this discussion of causal modeling techniques is that the results of such methods must be interpreted with caution, perhaps considerable caution. Despite their limitations, however, rigorous causal modeling has one distinct advantage: it tests for mediation as opposed to moderation (see Baron and Kenny, 1986, for a useful discussion of this distinction; also see Brett and James, 1984).

Process Manipulation: An Alternative Test of Hypothesized Mediators

Fortunately, there are ways of testing program theory other than causal modeling and related tests of hypothesized mediators. A second, more intrusive strategy involves active manipulation of process variables. In this approach, which can be called *process manipulation*, one seeks to stimulate or inhibit some hypothesized component of the process model. (Mark, 1986, differentiated the "blockage model," in which one seeks to inhibit a process mechanism, from the "enhancement model," in which one seeks to stimulate a process mechanism. For simplicity, these are treated together here as process manipulation.) Many examples of process manipulation come from medical research and other biological research traditions. For instance, a recent theory holds that cold symptoms occur because cold viruses stimulate production of kinins, a type of protein. Tests of this hypothesis involve administration of a bradykinin antagonist, which blocks kinins from having their effect (Kolata, 1987).

In many medical examples of process manipulation research, a theory of the cause of a disease is tested by introducing an agent, such as a vaccine, designed to block the causal process. Similarly, theory-based social interventions can be seen as tests of a proposed explanation of the causal chain underlying some social problem. For example, diversion programs for juvenile offenders can be seen as tests of the proposition that labeling a young offender as a criminal causes him or her to be more likely to commit crimes. The effectiveness of a theory-based intervention (for example, a juvenile diversion program based on labeling theory) supports the process explanation on which it is based (for example, a labeling theory approach to criminal behavior), just as the success of a vaccine supports the etiological theory on which it is based.

This means that program evaluation can sometimes be seen, in a broader perspective, as providing causal process research for theories of the etiology of social problems. This does not, however, excuse evaluators from doing research on the causal mechanism by which programs have their effects. First, social programs often are not explicitly based on any coherent theory of the etiology of a problem (Lipsey and others, 1985). Second, programs often include multiple components, addressing a problem in various ways, so it would be difficult to support a single causal theory simply from a program's success. Third, without evidence, one might not be confident that the effects of a program are due to the particular theory that spawned it: Relative to vaccinations, social programs are likely to be more diffuse in their effects and yet may also be more likely not to manipulate the theoretical process in question. In short, while program evaluation can *sometimes* be seen as testing process models of the etiology of social problems, even in such cases it is valuable to study the causal process by which the program has its effects.

Evaluators should be mindful of opportunities, however rare, for implementing the process manipulation approach. For example, imagine a program in which divorce cases are resolved not in the traditional court setting but instead through mediation. Social psychological research (for example, Thibaut and Walker, 1975) may suggest a program theory positing that the program would cause an increase in perceived control over the divorce procedures, and that this perceived control would lead to greater perceived fairness and thus to greater satisfaction. Process manipulation might be implemented in this case, for example, by making control over the procedures initially more salient to some disputants (for example, by drawing their attention to those features of the program that allow them to exercise control).

It is sometimes possible to conduct a process manipulation study as a "side study" (Saxe and Fine, 1979), that is, as a smaller study conducted adjunctly to the primary evaluation. Indeed, it is sometimes possible, while conducting an evaluation in the usual setting, to conduct a laboratory experiment in which the hypothesized mediator is manipulated. While one might have concern about the real-world applicability of such a laboratory-analog study, it might be an important link in the "many strands of evidence and reasoning" (Cronbach, 1982, p. 170) that are needed to draw recommendations for the future.

Further, when a process mechanism cannot be directly manipulated, evaluators should be on the lookout for naturally occurring instances of process manipulation. We return to this notion in a later section.

The process manipulation approach has at least three shortcomings. First, practical or ethical obstacles may make it impractical. Second, if the process manipulation inadvertently manipulates something other than, or in addition to, the intended process variable, inaccurate inferences may result. Third, the approach cannot differentiate between mediators and moderators (again, see Baron and Kenny, 1986, on this distinction). One strategy for dealing with this last problem is to conduct independent manipulations of the causal variable of interest, and of the presumed mediator, and to conduct causal modeling in conjunction.

Elaboration Does Not Require Assessment of Mediation

Both the causal modeling and process manipulation approaches deal, as directly as possible, with presumed mediational variables. Causal modeling does so through the observation and analysis of a possible mediator, and process manipulation through intervention. However, program theory can lead to elaborated predictions that do not involve a hypothesized mediator. Pattern matching can involve any of the elements of a causal inference: the cause, the outcomes, the persons or recipients of the treatment, the settings, and the time factor (Reichardt, 1988; Mark, 1986). Space prohibits detailed consideration of all such forms of elaboration, but mention and illustration of each of the preceding elements is provided.

Elaboration with Respect to the Cause. Program theories often imply predictions about differential effectiveness as a function of variations in treatment implementation or exposure. The most common such prediction is that more treatment exposures will result in stronger effects (Cook and Poole, 1982; Chen and Rossi, 1983, 1987); note, however, that selection artifacts will often threaten the validity of tests of this hypothesis (Mark, 1983).

Often program theory suggests other predictions that better differentiate the causal mechanism in question from its alternatives. For instance, program theory often specifies the causally efficacious components of a complex treatment. The *purification approach* to studying causal process (Mark, 1986) might then be applied. This approach can be illustrated by pharmacological research in which the investigator attempts to identify the active ingredient of a drug compound. That is, the investigator attempts to decompose a treatment and to isolate the component(s) that is (are) responsible for the desirable effect.

Evaluation may not support purification in an ideal form. Evaluators commonly do not have the authority or resources to modify the treatment or to test the effects of the various components of some complex treatment. However, three variations of the purification approach may be useful.

First, the researcher can examine naturally occurring or planned variations in the program across sites or across studies. If the treatment is effective when component X is present but ineffective when it is absent, one has evidence that component X is a causally active agent. One example is in Rossi, Berk, and Lenihan's (1980) evaluation of the Transitional Aid Research Project (TARP). TARP was a pilot program in which some newly released prisoners received financial aid in the form of unemployment insurance benefits, under the assumption that such aid would ease the transition back into everyday life and reduce the need to resume property crimes. Rossi, Berk, and Lenihan argued that beneficial effects were obscured by a work-disincentive effect. This argument was based partly on the results of another pilot study in which a form of payment that should not have had any work-disincentive effects was used, and in which a clear arrest reduction was observed. In this example, the decomposition of the treatment was based on a comparison across studies, but in many instances it may be possible to compare treatment composition across sites or across service deliverers.

A second variation of the purification approach is to conduct what Saxe and Fine (1979) call "side studies." As noted above in the context of process manipulation, sometimes even laboratory studies can be a useful component in a "fleet" of studies.

A third variation of the purification approach integrates purification and causal modeling techniques: One employs methods to estimate multiple causal paths from the treatment. The TARP evaluation again provides an illustration. Using structural equation techniques, Rossi, Berk, and Lenihan (1980) found that TARP payments had two counterbalancing effects: (1) controlling for level of postrelease employment, TARP payments lowered the number of arrests; however, (2) TARP payments also increased unemployment, so the arrest-averting effect was canceled out. More generally, if the evaluator can identify a separate causal path associated with each component of the treatment, it is in theory possible to assess the extent to which each component contributes to an observed effect. Unfortunately, with the current state of knowledge about social programs, it is often not possible to specify such a differentiated model with confidence. Further, the relevant analytical techniques are subject to a number of shortcomings, as noted above (see Zeisel's, 1982, critique of the TARP evaluation).

Another important form of elaboration or pattern matching with respect to treatment involves comparison across alternative representations of the same underlying causal construct. This strategy is widely known as *conceptual replication.* For instance, the case for cognitive dissonance theory was greatly bolstered by the fact that attitude change could be induced by a wide range of seemingly dissimilar causes (for example, counterattitudinal advocacy, postdecision evaluation of alternatives). Of course, as those familiar with the history of cognitive dissonance theory know, this example also illustrates one limit of pattern matching in general: It cannot differentiate between theories that predict the same pattern of results, as Bem's self-perception theory did for previous dissonance research (for a review of this research, see Cooper and Fazio, 1984).

Another instance of elaboration with the causal variable involves the functional relationship between the magnitude of the treatment variable and the effect. Well-developed process theories may make predictions of this sort. Chen and Rossi (1980, 1983) note such predictions, derived from economic theory, for income-maintenance experiments.

Pattern Matching with Respect to Outcomes. Pattern matching across outcomes can involve conceptual replication, as with the causal variable. Further, in many instances, different process theories predict different patterns across two or more dependent variables. For instance, in studying a persuasion technique called "low-balling," Cialdini, Cacioppo, Bassett, and Miller (1978) noted that some explanations for the effect predict a change in both behavior and attitude, while others predict a change in behavior but not attitude. By matching the observed pattern of effects across outcomes with the predicted patterns, the researchers argued that one process explanation was superior.

Trochim (1985) has emphasized that pattern matching underlies several quasi-experimental designs. Of relevance here, Trochim (1985) notes that the nonequivalent dependent-variables design (Cook and Campbell, 1979) relies explicitly on pattern matching across outcomes. While Cook and Campbell focus on the design's use to estimate the effects of a treatment, the present analysis emphasizes its use for probing causal process, whether in quasi-experimental or experimental design.

Marquart (this volume) provides an illustration of a form of pattern matching across outcomes, following the procedures suggested by Trochim (1985, 1989). However, in that approach the predicted pattern of outcomes is not based on a specified causal mechanism; rather, the "theoretical outcome pattern" is based on the expectations of practitioners who may use whatever "theories" they implicitly hold. Thus, that approach to pattern matching across outcomes does not test an explicit causal mechanism, but it could easily be expanded to do so.

Pattern Matching with Respect to Persons (or Other Units). Process theories sometimes predict differential patterns in terms of what types of respondents will be affected by the treatment. For example, a labeling theory analysis of juvenile diversion programs might lead to the following predictions: (1) diversion from the criminal justice system will decrease subsequent criminal activity among juveniles with few or no previous arrests, but (2) among juveniles with more extensive experience (for example, numerous arrests), diversion will not decrease criminal behavior because these youths will have already experienced labeling. If such a pattern were predicted by labeling theory and subsequently observed, the labeling theory interpretation of the programs's effects would be supported—to the extent that there are no other plausible process models that could also account for the pattern.

Sometimes when a program theory predicts that effects will vary across types of persons, this prediction represents a naturally occurring process manipulation. For example, consider the hypothesis that a psycho-educational intervention aimed at reducing the length of hospital stays (Devine and Cook, 1983) works because it gives patients information that allows them to anticipate events and experiences, which in turn allows them to prepare for and attempt to control their responses (in what otherwise can be a setting that undermines a sense of efficacy). But some patients—those who use denial or do not believe they can control their responses in aversive settings—may not use information in the desired way. The patients' preexisting tendencies may represent a naturally occurring "blocking agent." More generally, by identifying respondent or situational characteristics that should inhibit (or enhance) a hypothesized effect, and by seeing if that variable interacts with the treatment, an evaluator can test the program theory. Of course, the test's validity depends on whether the respondent or situational characteristic does affect the hypothesized process mechanism (and not others).

Pattern Matching with Respect to Settings. Process theories sometimes predict the circumstances under which an effect will occur. In the research on low-balling cited above (Cialdini, Cacioppo, Bassett, and Miller, 1978), some process theories predicted an effect only when people perceived that they had free choice in their selections, while other process theories predicted an effect whether or not free choice was present. By comparing the observed pattern across choice–no choice conditions, with the alternative predicted patterns, Cialdini, Cacioppo, Bassett, and Miller (1978) were able to endorse one process explanation over the others.

Pattern Matching Across Time. Alternative process models sometimes make different predictions about an effect as a function of time. This is common in cognitive psychology, where response time measures are widely used to differentiate alternative process models. For example, in an evaluation of psychotherapy, a placebo explanation might predict a sudden, relatively steady effect over time, while an alternative model based on cognitive theory might predict a gradual increase in effect.

Process theories also sometimes predict different effects based on the timing of the treatment. For example, Srull and Wyer (1980) studied the effect of manipulated accessibility of cognitive categories (for example, kind) on subjects' impressions of target persons. Srull and Wyer claimed that, according to the relevant psychological theory, this so-called priming should have an effect if it occurred before exposure to each target but not if it occurred after; in contrast, they argued, a demand characteristics argument predicts an effect whether the priming occurred before or after exposure to the target.

Conclusion. The forms of elaboration or pattern matching described above, which do not involve a hypothesized mediator, share the same shortcomings, Rigorous application of the pattern-matching approach requires that competing process models have clear, precise, and different predictions, whether those predictions are made with respect to cause, outcomes, persons, settings, or time. Process models for programs—indeed, social science theory in general—is often not so well developed. Consider two examples cited above. First, if we disagree with Srull and Wyer's (1980) contention that priming theory and demand characteristics imply a different pattern of results, we are not convinced that the observed results strengthen the priming interpretation. A pattern-matching approach can do no better than the process models on which it is based, and if the process models are unclear, ambiguous, or subject to simple post hoc revision, clear differentiation of models may not result. Second, in the attitude change literature, pattern matching across treatments once seemed to point clearly to dissonance as a causal process; but after Bem offered self-perception as an alternative interpretation, the implications of the pattern of data for causal process no loger seemed so clear. Pattern matching may seem to support one causal mechanism, but such support is tentative, for better explanations may be forthcoming.

Confident conclusions based on a pattern-matching strategy also require elimination of other interpretations of the observed pattern. For instance, if, as predicted, we observe an effect in one group but not another, we must rule out alternative explanations such as differential statistical power.

Despite these limits, we can and should attempt to increase our thoughtful application of pattern-matching strategies, if for no other reason than it makes us think explicitly about the implications of our program theories and address any ambiguities they may have. Moreover, in many instances pattern matching, if carefully applied, provides a valuable test of program theories. In addition, pattern-matching logic can be helpful for discovering process after the fact; that is, when unexpected differences are observed across measures or subgroups, the logic of pattern matching can help us to deduce the process responsible.

Review and Conclusions about Methods for Testing Program Theory

Several approaches to the study of causal process have been described in this chapter. Causal modeling and process manipulation focus directly on the presumed mediating variables, causal modeling through measurement and process manipulation through intervention. Causal modeling methods can in principle assess mediation, but they are subject to limitations of causal inference. Process manipulation methods are strong with respect to causal inference, assuming accurate manipulation of the presumed process variable, but cannot alone differentiate mediation from moderation.

The pattern-matching approach has several other variants, corresponding to the elements of a causal inference across which a pattern is predicted. All pattern-matching approaches gain explanatory strength to the extent that one process model uniquely predicts some pattern of results, while (any) competing models do not. This requirement leads to the most serious shortcomings of a pattern-matching approach: Social science theories are commonly not so precise, unique, and clear, and often we simply have not yet created the superior, competing model (Cook and Campbell, 1979, esp. pp. 20-25).

Given the shortcomings of various process methods, what do we do? Probably, the best answer is to be what Cook (1985) and his associates call "critical multiplists." In part, this entails seeking evidence from multiple forms of tests of program theory and critically examining the potential bias in each test. Conclusions about program theory are then likely to be based on more than single studies. Thus, pattern matching across studies, findings from more basic research, process results from within studies, and a complex chain of reasoning are likely to bolster argument about causal process (Cronbach, 1982). But reasonable conclusions about causal mechanisms are unlikely unless evaluators attempt to test program theory within evaluations. Tests of program theory, as suggested in the present chapter, can take a variety of forms, involving elaboration with respect to the mediators, the cause, the outcomes, the persons receiving the program, the settings, and time. Evaluators will maximize their ability to test program theory by considering all of the options available. And the full benefits of program theory will not accrue unless program theories are tested.

References

Baron, R. M., and Kenny, D. A. "The Moderator-Mediator Variable Distinction in Social Psychological Research: Conceptual, Strategic, and Statistical Considerations." *Journal of Personality and Social Psychology*, 1986, 51, 1173-1182.
Baumrind, D. "Specious Causal Attributions in the Social Sciences: The Reformu-

lated Stepping-Stone Theory of Heroin Use as Exemplar." *Journal of Personality and Social Psychology*, 1983, *45*, 189–198.

Bickman, L. "Improving Established Statewide Programs: A Component Theory of Evaluation." *Evaluation Review*, 1985, *9*, 189–208.

Bickman, L. "The Functions of Program Theory." In L. Bickman (ed.), *Using Program Theory in Evaluation*. New Directions for Program Evaluation, no. 33. San Francisco: Jossey-Bass, 1987a.

Bickman, L. (ed.). *Using Program Theory in Evaluation*. New Directions for Program Evaluation, no. 33. San Francisco: Jossey-Bass, 1987b.

Brett, J. M., and James, L. R. "Mediators, Moderators, and Tests for Mediation." *Journal of Applied Psychology*, 1984, *69*, 307–321.

Campbell, D. T. "Pattern Making as an Essential in Distal Knowing." In K. R. Hammond (ed.), *The Psychology of Egon Brunswik*. New York: Holt, Rinehart & Winston, 1966.

Campbell, D. T. "Degrees of Freedom and the Case Study." *Comparative Political Studies*, 1975, *8*, 178–193.

Chen, H.-T. (ed.). Special issue on "The Theory-Driven Perspective." *Evaluation and Program Planning*, 1989, *12*, entire issue.

Chen, H.-T., and Rossi, P. H. "The Multi-Goal, Theory-Driven Approach to Evaluation: A Model Linking Basic and Applied Social Science." *Social Forces*, 1980, *59*, 106–122.

Chen, H.-T., and Rossi, P. H. "Evaluating with Sense: The Theory-Driven Approach." *Evaluation Review*, 1983, *7*, 238–302.

Chen, H.-T., and Rossi, P. H. "The Theory-Driven Approach to Validity." *Evaluation and Program Planning*, 1987, *10*, 95–103.

Cialdini, R. B., Cacioppo, J. T., Bassett, R., and Miller, J. A. "Low-Ball Procedure for Producing Compliance: Commitment Then Cost." *Journal of Personality and Social Psychology*, 1978, *36*, 463–476.

Cochran, W. G. "The Planning of Observational Studies of Human Populations." *Journal of the Royal Statistical Society*, 1965, *182*, 234–255.

Cook, T. D. "Post-Positivist Critical Multiplism." In R. L. Shotland and M. M. Mark (eds.), *Social Science and Social Policy*. Newbury Park, Calif.: Sage, 1985.

Cook, T. D., and Campbell, D. T. *Quasi-Experimentation: Design and Analysis Issues for Field Settings*. Skokie, Ill.: Rand McNally, 1979.

Cook, T. J., and Poole, W. K. "Treatment Implementation and Statistical Power: A Research Note." *Evaluation Review*, 1982, *6*, 425–430.

Cooper, J., and Fazio, R. H. "A New Look at Dissonance Theory." In L. Berkowitz (ed.), *Advances in Experimental Social Psychology*. Vol. 17. Orlando, Fla.: Academic Press, 1984.

Cordray, D. S. "Optimizing Validity in Program Research: An Elaboration of Chen and Rossi's Theory-Driven Approach." *Evaluation and Program Planning*, 1989, *12*, 379–385.

Costner, H. L. "The Validity of Conclusions in Evaluation Research: A Further Development of Chen and Rossi's Theory-Driven Approach." *Evaluation and Program Planning*, 1989, *12*, 345–353.

Cronbach, L. J. *Designing Evaluations of Educational and Social Programs*. San Francisco: Jossey-Bass, 1982.

Devine, E. C., and Cook, T. D. "Effects of Psycho-Educational Interventions on Length of Hospital Stay: A Meta-Analytic Review of Thirty-Four Studies." In R. J. Light (ed.), *Evaluation Studies Review Annual*. Vol. 8. Newbury Park, Calif.: Sage, 1983.

Freedman, D. A. "As Others See Us: A Case Study in Path Analysis." *Journal of Educational Statistics*, 1987, *12*, 101-128.
Judd, C. M., and Kenny, D. A. "Process Analysis: Estimating Mediation in Treatment Evaluations." *Evaluation Review*, 1981, *5*, 602-619.
Kolata, G. "Clever Strategy Shows Promise Against Colds." *New York Times*, Oct. 6, 1987, pp. Cl, C6.
Lipsey, M. W., Crosse, S., Dunkle, J., Pollard, J., and Stobart, G. "Evaluation: The State of the Art and the Sorry State of the Science." New Directions for Program Evaluation, no. 27. San Francisco: Jossey-Bass, 1985.
Lipsey, M. W., and Pollard, J. A. "Driving Toward Theory in Program Evaluation: More Models to Choose from." *Evaluation and Program Planning*, 1989, *12*, 317-328.
Mark, M. M. "Treatment Implementation, Statistical Power, and Internal Validity." *Evaluation Review*, 1983, *7*, 543-549.
Mark, M. M. "Validity Typologies and the Logic and Practice of Quasi-Experimentation." In W.M.K. Trochim (ed.), *Advances in Quasi-Experimental Design and Analysis*. San Francisco: Jossey-Bass, 1986.
Platt, J. R. "Strong Inference." *Science*, 1964, *146*, 347-353.
Reichardt, C. S. "Estimating Effects." Unpublished manuscript, Department of Psychology, University of Denver, 1988.
Rosenbaum, P. R. "From Association to Causation in Observational Studies: The Role of Tests of Strongly Ignorable Treatment Assignment." *Journal of the American Statistical Association*, 1984, *79*, 40-48.
Rossi, P. H., Berk, R. A., and Lenihan, K. J. *Money, Work, and Crime*. Orlando, Fla.: Academic Press, 1980.
Saxe, L., and Fine, M. "Expanding Our View of Controls in Evaluation." In L. E. Datta and R. Perloff (eds.), *Improving Evaluations*. Newbury Park, Calif.: Sage, 1979.
Srull, T. K., and Wyer, R. S. "Category Accessibility and Social Perception: Some Implications for the Study of Person Memory and Interpersonal Judgments." *Journal of Personality and Social Psychology*, 1980, *38*, 841-856.
Thibaut, J. W., and Walker, L. *Procedural Justice: A Psychological Analysis*. Hillsdale, N.J.: Erlbaum, 1975.
Trochim, W.M.K. "Pattern Matching, Construct Validity, and Conceptualization in Program Evaluation." *Evaluation Review*, 1985, *9*, 575-604.
Trochim, W.M.K. "Outcome Pattern Matching and Program Theory." *Evaluation and Program Planning*, 1989, *12*, 355-366.
Zeisel, H. "Disagreement over the Evaluation of a Controlled Experiment." *American Journal of Sociology*, 1982, *88*, 378-389.

Melvin M. Mark is an associate professor and associate head of the Department of Psychology at The Pennsylvania State University, University Park. He is coeditor of Evaluation Studies Review Annual, Vol. 3, Social Science and Social Policy, *and* Multiple Methods in Program Evaluation *(NDPE, no. 35).*

Path analysis is an effective causal modeling approach for explicating and testing both program theory and program impact.

Using Path Analysis to Develop and Evaluate Program Theory and Impact

Nick L. Smith

In spite of earlier calls (for example, Fitz-Gibbon and Morris, 1975) for evaluators to design more theory-based studies, only in the past few years has there been significant attention devoted to the role of program theory in evaluation (for example, Chen and Rossi, 1983; Cook and Shadish, 1986; Shadish and Reichardt, 1987; Bickman, 1987; Trochim, 1989).

With the increased interest in the role of program theory in evaluation has come a search for alternative means of dealing with program theory. One approach that has been suggested is the use of causal modeling (for example, McClintock, 1987; Mark, this volume). Path analysis is a form of causal modeling suited to the development and evaluation of program theory. This chapter provides a brief overview of path analysis and reports the results of earlier attempts to use path analysis to explicate and study program theory.

Path Analysis Procedures

Path analysis is one of several causal modeling procedures that might be used to represent the test program theory in evaluation. Path analysis is not a single

This chapter draws heavily from two prior, generally overlooked, publications, Smith and Murray (1978) and Murray and Smith (1979), representing the joint work of Stephen L. Murray and me. I am solely responsible for any errors in the current rendition.

statistical procedure but rather a collection of ways of analyzing data using models to depict the influence of one set of variables on another (Spaeth, 1975). Although the techniques of path analysis have been developed primarily for use with nonexperimental data, they can also be applied to experimental, cross-sectional, and longitudinal data. Path analysis consists of making explicit both the theoretical formulations of causal relationships within the program and any related assumptions, and subjecting them to empirical test. Path analysis thus forces a sharpening and testing of both the logical and empirical bases underlying programmatic causal claims.

Murray and Smith (1979, p. 388) summarize the methods of path analysis as follows:

> Path analysis can be characterized as relating primarily to the analysis of nonexperimental data and the absence of laboratory or experimental controls, as employing latent variables that are implied in the relationships with the observable variables, and as utilizing a systems orientation reflected in the use of sets of interacting relational equations. It involves the construction of explicitly formulated alternative structural (causal) models that imply patterns or relationships among variables. The underlying causal reasoning is made explicit in the form of path diagrams and structural equations. Regression analysis is then used to construct "path coefficients" (beta weights). Models inconsistent with the data are rejected, while those not rejected are viewed as plausible causal patterns to be studied further. Causation cannot be unambiguously demonstrated using these techniques, but some causal patterns can be rendered more believable than others.

Path analysis originated in genetics with the work of Wright (1921, 1960) and was introduced to the social sciences primarily as a result of Blalock's (1964, 1971) and Duncan's (1966) use of causal modeling in sociology. General discussions of path analysis are provided in Duncan (1966), Land (1969), Blalock (1971), Werts and Linn (1971), and Spaeth (1975). See Murray and Smith (1979) for a discussion of the use of path analysis in program evaluation, including an overview and introduction to the method, an extended example, and numerous references to procedures and studies of path analysis (see also Smith and Murray, 1978).

The first step in a path analysis is to construct a path diagram, which is a graphic display of the order in which variables are assumed to affect one another. The variables in a path diagram are referred to as either *endogenous* (dependent on other variables) or *exogenous* (affecting endogenous variables). Multiple stages of causation, reciprocal causation, and the reduction of causal influences into direct and indirect effects (for example, through intervening variables) can be represented in path analysis. Regression equations mathematically representing the causal diagram are then systematically generated and solved. The theory of the program being evaluated can thus be diagrammatically and mathematically represented and tested for its fit with observed data.

Uses and Examples

A major strength of path analysis as a statistical procedure for developing and testing program theory is that it is one of the few means available for mathematically modeling complex and innovative program. Other multivariate approaches do not provide a means of simultaneously testing both the rationale and the effectiveness of a program. Further, path analysis techniques enable evaluators to test both direct and indirect program effects within the same study, and they force the consideration of alternative program theories.

Murray and Smith (1979) provide an example of the use of path analysis within a nonrandomized control group design to evaluate a teacher-training system. they examined the theoretical relationships among teacher characteristics (age, sex), class size, training level, teacher orientation, and teacher classroom behavior. Their path analysis results supported the basic training rationale that linked teacher orientation to teacher classroom behavior, but the results showed that the training was not a sufficiently strong treatment to change the teachers' orientations. By contrast, an analysis of covariance conducted on the same data showed only that the training was ineffective. Thus, while non-path analysis procedures also indicated nonsignificant training results, the path analysis identified that the problem was not in the training rationale but rather in the weakness of treatment.

Smith and Murray (1978) cite a number of strengths of path analysis, including its utility at a heuristic, logical, or statistical level. In developing and testing program theory in evaluation, path analysis can be used (1) to identify and make explicit developer and stakeholder conceptions on the program being evaluated, (2) to construct an iteratively refined, graphic representation reflecting consensus on program theory, (3) to provide a model of the program on which to base subsequent evaluation design decisions (that is, path analysis ties the evaluating rationale to the development rationale), (4) to test program impact, (5) to test program process, (6) to explicate and test program assumptions and theory, and (7) to explicate and test alternative program theories (for example, to search for another model that better fits the observed data).

Smith (1981) provides an example of the heuristic and logical uses of path analysis in developing and assessing program theory (that is, he uses [1]-[4] listed above). He reports on a two-year evaluation of a large program designed to increase the participation of rural citizens in local school activities. Starting with vague statements of program interrelations, the evaluation staff iteratively developed a path analysis model of the complex, multilayered community-intervention program being constructed. The use of the graphic display (that is, path diagram) helped development staff clarify unrecognized points of internal disagreement and construct a logically stronger program theory. The path analysis modeling procedures also facilitated the design of a modular evaluation design that assessed program effectiveness at a few key points in the intervention and proved robust in spite of subsequent cuts in evaluation funding.

Caution and Conclusion

A number of technical and pragmatic assumptions have to be met in order to apply statistical path analysis procedures. For example, there must be a clearly defined causal system that includes all relevant variables, the model must specify the temporal ordering of variables in terms of theory, and the variables must be measured with a minimal number of errors (see Murray and Smith, 1979, for additional requirements).

Further, there are several problems to contend with in applying path analysis, as is also the case with other causal modeling (see Mark, this volume). The procedures are more costly and time consuming than simple pre-post testing, and they require collaborative work with developers to specify structural models that reflect program theory. In addition, although the techniques can be used to model complex systems, strong a priori rationales are needed to restrict the number of structural options (a five-variable system can be portrayed in 1,048,576 possible configurations; Young, 1977). Also, the use of path analysis to evaluate developmental programs may require the construction of original instrumentation, the uniqueness of which limits the generalizability of theoretical conclusions. Some time ago, Spaeth (1975), Feldman (1975), and Pedhazur (1975) discussed additional but now well-known, technical problems in the use of path analysis, such as specification errors, measurement errors, and multicollinearity (see Smith and Murray, 1978, for a brief summary of these).

There are practical and technical difficulties in conducting path analyses, but the procedures provide a unique means of developing and testing both program theory and impact. Although useful as a heuristic or logical tool, as a statistical approach path analysis can provide empirical evidence for the testing and refining of program theory, thereby achieving a full integration of development and evaluation in the construction of effective programs.

References

Bickman, L. (ed.). *Using Program Theory in Evaluation.* New Directions for Program Evaluation, no. 33. San Francisco: Jossey-Bass, 1987.
Blalock, H. M. *Causal Inferences in Non-Experimental Research.* Chapel Hill: University of North Carolina Press, 1964.

Blalock, H. M. *Causal Models in the Social Sciences.* Chicago: Aldine, 1971.

Chen, H.-T., and Rossi, P. H. "Evaluating with Sense: The Theory-Driven Approach." *Evaluation Review,* 1983, 7, 283-302.

Cook, T. D., and Shadish, W. R. "Program Evaluation: The Worldly Science." *Annual Review of Psychology,* 1986, 37, 193-232.

Duncan, O. D. "Path Analysis: Sociological Examples." *American Journal of Sociology,* 1966, 72, 1-16.

Feldman, J. "Considerations in the Use of Causal-Correlational Techniques in Applied Psychology." *Journal of Applied Psychology,* 1975, 60 (6), 663-670.

Fitz-Gibbon, C. T., and Morris, L. L. "Theory-Based Evaluation." *Evaluation Comment,* 1975, 5, 1-4.

Land, K. C. "Principles of Path Analysis." In E. F. Borgatta and G. W. Bohrnstedt (eds.), *Sociological Methodology.* San Francisco: Jossey-Bass, 1969.

McClintock, C. "Conceptual and Action Heuristics: Tools for the Evaluator." In L. Bickman (ed.), *Using Program Theory in Evaluation.* New Directions for Program Evaluation, no. 33. San Francisco: Jossey-Bass, 1987.

Murray, S. L., and Smith, N. L. "Causal Research on Teacher Training." In H. J. Walberg (ed.), *Educational Environments and Effects: Evaluation, Policy, and Productivity.* Berkeley, Calif.: McCutchan, 1979.

Pedhazur, E. J. "Analytic Methods in Studies of Educational Effects." In F. N. Kerlinger (ed.), *Review of Research in Education.* Vol. 3. Itasca, Ill.: Peacock, 1975.

Shadish, W. R., and Reichardt, C. S. (eds.). *Evaluation Studies Review Annual.* Vol. 12. Newbury Park, Calif.: Sage, 1987.

Smith, N. L. "Evaluability Assessment: A Retrospective Illustration and Review." *Educational Evaluation and Policy Analysis,* 1981, 3 (1), 77-82.

Smith, N. L., and Murray, S. L. *The Use of Path Analysis in Program Evaluation.* Occasional Paper Series No. 23. Bloomington, Ind.: Phi Delta Kappa, Center on Evaluation, Development, and Research, 1978.

Spaeth, J. L. "Path Analysis." In D. J. Amick and H. J. Walberg (eds.), *Introductory Multivariate Analysis.* Berkeley, Calif.: McCutchan, 1975.

Trochim, W.M.K. "Concept Mapping for Evaluation and Planning." *Evaluation and Program Planning,* 1989, 12 (1), 1-111.

Werts, C. E., and Linn, R. L. "Path Analysis: Psychological Examples." *Psychological Bulletin,* 1971, 74, 193-212.

Wright, S. "Correlation and Causation." *Journal of Agricultural Research,* 1921, 20, 557-585.

Wright, S. "Data Coefficients and Path Regressions: Alternate or Complementary Concepts?" *Biometrics,* 1960, 16, 189-202.

Young, J. W. "The Function of Theory in a Dilemma of Path Analysis." *Journal of Applied Psychology,* 1977, 62, 108-110.

Nick L. Smith is an associate professor in the School of Education at Syracuse University, Syracuse, New York. His primary research interest is the methodology of applied field research and evaluation.

PART THREE

Applications

Measures of program quality can be derived using component program theory and consensus building with panels of experts.

Using Program Theory to Describe and Measure Program Quality

Leonard Bickman, Keith A. Peterson

Social programs are implemented to effect policy-designated change, hopefully through high-quality, high-impact interventions. However, most program evaluations that assess impact are often characterized as "black box" evaluations because they emphasize measurement of outcomes and generally disregard measurement of the quality of the program, despite its centrality to understanding successful program operation (Lipsey and others, 1985). A primary reason for this neglect may be the operational, as well as philosophical, difficulties in defining and measuring quality. This chapter argues that the measurement of program quality is essential to successful program evaluation, and that the description and measurement of quality emerges from program theory. By explicating program theory, evaluators can both identify and prioritize dimensions of program quality.

The Quality Emphasis

Quality is of significant interest to the social services and to the service industries in general. For example, responding to the skyrocketing costs of health care, policymakers have recently found that emphasizing efficiency and cost factors have led to effective new standards of service delivery quality (Califano, 1986). In education, scholars have long debated the use of indicators of quality teaching and learning (Dewey, 1938; Nichols, 1989). Business organizations frequently focus on the issue of quality in their efforts to improve their competitiveness (for example, the slogan "Quality is Job One"). Despite such interest in these diverse contexts, the quantitative measurement of quality has not received its deserved attention in the evaluation field. However,

NEW DIRECTIONS FOR PROGRAM EVALUATION, no. 47, Fall 1990 © Jossey-Bass Inc., Publishers we believe that the increasing attention to program theory will lead to new interest in, and development of, measures of quality for program evaluation. We show here how such measures hold the promise of providing more efficient and less costly evaluations.

Defining Quality

Defining quality is no small feat. Phaedrus, the mythical figure, is said to have been driven mad by the metaphysical complexities of the issue (Pirsig, 1974). The lesson we take from this myth is that we should be constrained by our own epistemological beliefs, lest we suffer a similar fate. Our reviews of the philosophy and research of a broad range of disciplines have helped us, however, to identify some of the relevant features of quality. First, we assume that quality is a value statement that is interpreted by the observer. Second, this value statement indicates a general preference for or favorable disposition toward an object. Third, quality is neither wholly subjective nor objective but depends on the relationship between the object and the individual making the judgment (quality is partly inherent in the object and thus is present whether people notice it or not). Last, while there may be differences between individuals in how they define quality, there can be a consensus about relative quality.

Program theory guides the selection of a strategy for measuring quality. The evaluator must make decision rules concerning what constitutes the elements of the program theory, and how the linkages between those elements will be assessed. In health services research, Donabedian (1966, 1980) suggests that quality assessment should include analysis of structure, process, and outcomes. Others suggest that criteria selection depends on the purpose of the assessment (Brook, Kamberg, and Lohr, 1983). For instance, low-cost evaluations may frequently focus on identifying outliers, that is, those programs or services failing minimal standards. This identification typically requires fairly simple criteria and assessment methods (documentation of legal sanctions, complaints, and so on). If a model program is being studied in order to find ways of improving average programs, however, more sophisticated and sensitive measures may be necessary (for example, measures of process and multiple indicators of effectiveness).

A second set of decisions regards setting priorities about which components of the intervention process are most relevant or important. This prioritization is critical because it allows a more focused perspective on where and how to improve the program, and it indicates how to identify the worst problems and best features of the program. Prioritization concerns ranking problem areas in terms of their impact on program operation and intervention effectiveness. Some work has addressed prioritization in health services (Vuori, 1980; Brook, Davies, and Kamberg, 1980); however, little information is available about which criteria are best used to identify the most pressing problems.

It seems to us that an important misconception is that prioritization is usually considered as a methodological question rather than as a theory question. Program theory, by definition, should tell us not only of what the program consists but also something about the dynamics of the program, what features are most important in regulating its functioning, and what outcomes are important. Chen (this volume) describes both normative theory, which entails a prescriptive notion about what the program *should* do, and causative theory, which entails a description of *how* the innovation works. This information is integrated through reasoning and valuing, using knowledge of cultural beliefs and norms, public policy, and research. For instance, tests of causal models indicate which relations in models are the strongest, in which direction they operate (A $\rightarrow$ B, A $\leftarrow$ B, or A $\leftrightarrow$ B), and whether the relationship is positive or negative. These findings could thus be used to prioritize these variables in the context of evaluation. Thus, quality measurement should move from selection of general dimensions of a program that relates to quality via theory, to the description of program characteristics within those dimensions. Then, valuing of individual characteristics as quality indicators can narrow the research focus and lead to the selection of a theory-driven assessment method.

Program theory is essential for deciding what to measure in a program, as well as for valuing or determining the importance of different program characteristics. With a good sense of program theory, the evaluator can move to observing program process and operation, rather than focusing on simple (and frequently uninterpretable) outcomes. Further, program theory forces the evaluator to adapt a normative point of view. In other words, it clarifies the set of perspectives on which the evaluation of quality will be based. For instance, applied social science models are often developed from a normative perspective: models of mental health care delivery often make certain assumptions about the nature of what is good for recipients (for example, family preservation, least-restrictive services). These statements are used to describe a system, and for the evaluator they reflect program values from the stakeholder perspective. Providing least-restrictive services means placing the client in the treatment environment least disruptive to his or her normal social system, reflecting the value accrued by the client. Least-restrictive services, however, also reflect a cost benefit because they typically refer to out-patient versus more expensive in-patient services. Thus, statements about, and descriptions of, a program from a theoretical model pinpoint valued processes and outcomes. Identifying the program's primary perspective(s) should lead to the ranking of components of a program in terms of their ability to contribute to program goals. Before addressing the issue of selecting quality criteria, we briefly introduce some ideas about the nature of quality.

Quality and Improvement

Quality as used here is a response to clearly labeled characteristics of a program. This approach can be contrasted with mechanistic models such as quality-control systems that do not require human judgment. Such models were originally designed to ensure minimal standards of care, but they do little to discriminate average quality from high quality. Referring to medical care, Berwick (1989) contrasts what he calls the "theory of bad apples" with the "theory of continuous improvement." His position, though it focuses on achieving rather than evaluating quality, informs this discussion. In the theory of bad apples, quality is achieved through inspection and the discovery and removal of bad apples. It implies minimal thresholds for acceptability and a search for low-quality outliers. Berwick believes that this approach leads to problems such as gaming the system and blaming the victim and thus to no real improvement in quality.

Alternatively, the theory of continuous improvement is based on management principles applied in Japan (Deming, 1982, 1986; Juran, 1964; Juran, Gryna, and Bingham, 1979). The key principle here is that one should not focus on the poor-quality outlier but rather on the average producer. Shifting the quality curve of the entire process slightly upward produces significantly more productivity than simply trying to cut off the lower end of the distribution. Indeed, minimal standards often become ceilings instead of floors and prevent the achievement of excellence. As Berwick notes, to institute this process in health care we need to understand the complex process of health care. This principle should apply to every comprehensive evaluation. To measure quality, the evaluator must have a clear sense of the program theory, because from theory flows the description of the program; and description identifies what should be measured in the program.

Preschool Programs: An Application

We recently developed an instrument—the Component Quality Checklist (CQC)—to use in an evaluation of the quality of preschool programs for handicapped and at-risk children. A decision was made to focus on developing quality measures of certain key program components and to validate the instrument using expert opinions and an effectiveness study of key components.

To illustrate, we consider here the evaluation of the *transition* component. Transition refers to the preparation required for the child to move from the preschool program to school. Our reviews of the literature suggested that few evaluations have been conducted dealing with transition services, but that there was increasing interest in that component (for example, a Transition Task Force was formed by the Tennessee Early Intervention Network for Children with Handicaps, as well as a national consortium of Handicapped Children's Early Educational Programs). Thus, we needed to develop a theory about transition services, addressing both causal theory, in terms of how the services worked, and normative theory, in terms of what they should do.

Our theory of transition services was developed from the social science literature, interviews with experts, interviews with stakeholders of preschool programs, and our experience as evaluators. A depiction of the final model is presented in Figure 1. In developing that program theory, we first identified and specified the values associated with transition services from the relevant perspectives (social science and stakeholder). This included specification of the initial transition problem at all possible levels (individual, organizational, system) and the change strategies on which the existing transition service were based, as well as explication of the nature of the implementation of a transition system and desirable outcomes of that system.

Our research suggested that children and families frequently encounter a number of critical and stressful points in the children's development. One of the most difficult of these points is when children enter school. Children must cope with major changes in their environments in terms of dealing with staff, different peers, new teaching methods and classrooms, activities schedules, and so on. Parents who have had their children in special education preschool programs face comparisons of their own child to the other children. The hoped for success of an early intervention program may not have materialized and allowed the child to catch up to age-level peers. At the same time, both parents and child are being asked to leave the known and hopefully supportive staff and program for an unknown and untested environment. How the parents react to the transition is assumed to be critical to the child's success. It is further assumed that high-quality transition services can assist this process.

The basic concerns of the children, parents, and teachers in the transition process focus on the children's placement, progress, and adjustment and on the total transition process itself. Central to an effective transition is the participation of the parents in the education process. A high-quality transition process should thus support communication among the children's teachers about skill levels as well as specific teaching, learning, and motivational strategies. Such communication should promote each child's positive adjustment and progress and prevent unnecessary regression.

Once the normative perspective was completed, we described the program, along with the (causal) relationships between program components. From this brief theoretical statement, we then developed comprehensive descriptions of transition functions and activities.

Figure 1. Model of Preschool Program, Highlighting the Transition Component

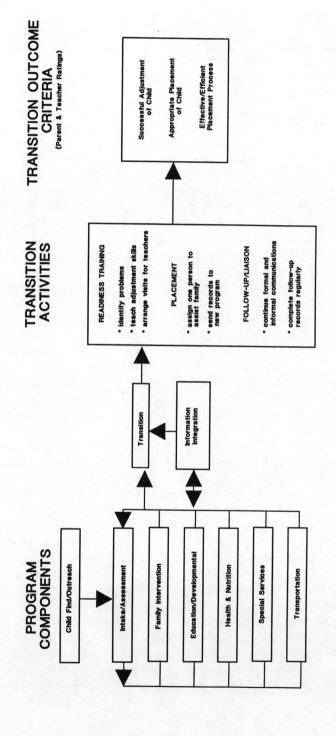

Describing Services—A Component Approach

The component approach to evaluation is a systematic method of describing programs (Bickman, 1985). This approach builds on the idea that programs are a collection of components consisting of related activities and directed at attaining some goal. Associated with each component are purpose statements and a number of functions relating how goals are reached. We used the following purpose statement of transition: "Transition entails preparing the family and the child to move to a new program, assisting in finding the appropriate placement, and remaining in contact with the family and the program's personnel after the changeover." The functions and activities included the following:

Function 1. *Readiness training:* identify specific transition problems, teach children skills and behaviors that will facilitate their adjustment to the proposed placement, teach parents activities to do at home that relate to entry into the proposed placement, and arrange visit to current placement for teacher and parents.

Function 2. *Placement:* assign a specific person to assist each family, assist family in finding an appropriate placement, and send pertinent information to new program.

Function 3. *Follow-up/liaison:* continue formal and informal communication between present and former teachers, and complete systematic written follow-up records at scheduled intervals.

With a comprehensive topography of the component, we know not only the degree to which components goals are being met but also why they are functioning successfully. This information is especially useful when the evaluation is part of an effort to replicate a model program elsewhere. Further, by knowing more about the internal processes of a specific program component, we gain the opportunity for a better understanding of how components influence each other. For example, effective transition services are largely dependent on appropriate family intervention services. If a family is not helped to function effectively as a unit during involvement in the program, it is doubtful that the transition will be smooth. In terms of program quality then, consideration of the contributive value of any component is important for directing the assessment method.

Clearly, a large number of activities and subactivities can and should be generated in gaining an exhaustive picture of components. For example, our efforts to develop a topography of family intervention services as a component yielded six functions and forty activities. Such an exhaustive description is necessary to provide a complete representation of the program, and to sensitize the development of the evaluation instrument to context-specific issues or activities that may be critical, yet not readily apparent to the evaluator. Thus, with a description of the program in hand, the second step in developing the CQC was to prioritize those functions and activities in some meaningful fashion.

Building Consensus About Quality Criteria

Once a component is well described, it is necessary to identify those functions and activities that are most important to measuring quality. The first step is the identification of the dimensions or descriptive characteristics of the activity that is of interest. For example, the relevant dimensions of quality transition services included degree of availability, degree of participation, type of provider, group size, frequency, duration, and type of setting. The dimensions should logically flow from the type of component or service under investigation and be clearly operationalized. Examples of other dimensions include treatment intensity, staff-client match, and staff motivation and commitment.

Following the selection of quality dimensions, the dimensions must be prioritized because it is unlikely that each dimension carries equal weight in predicting program effectiveness. One approach to valuing or prioritizing these dimensions involves consensus building. These methods usually involve soliciting opinions from experts, building consensus, and applying these criteria to specific cases. The use of consensual valuing is the strongest approach to developing quality indicators because it maximizes the capacity to satisfy the largest number of constituencies.

Our approach has been to choose a small number of key program components and then validate our prioritization method using these components. For example, in the preschool program we focused on the family intervention and transition services as components of interest. The choice of components should be based on their centrality to the program, so as to maximize the effectiveness of the measures for indicating the level of quality associated with a program. This approach uses panels of experts to rank the importance of the relevant activities and subactivities. In the first stage of developing the CQC, a panel of two hundred practitioner and academic experts judged the importance of various activities. However, panels may be smaller if attention is paid to selecting a representative sample of experts.

We then used the ratings to construct the quality assessment instrument. Activities were weighted to select their importance to component quality and overall quality. Various measurement techniques can be used to accomplish this task. A simple approach is to use ipsative (ranking) scales, where elements are ranked in relation to one another. In the preschool evaluation, a panel of experts was asked to distribute a total of one hundred points among the functions for each component. More important functions were thus given greater weight, and so on. Then, reliability coefficients can be computed among the raters and between groups of raters (for example, between practitioners and researchers). Once the rankings are achieved, the results can be used to derive a number of quality indicators.

In the second stage, we validated the instrument using a known-groups technique. This validation technique used a series of profiles from high- and low-quality program components as defined by our rating instrument. A total of thirty-two programs in Tennessee were selected, sixteen that had high-quality transition services and sixteen with low-quality components. The quality rankings of these thirty-two preschool programs were obtained from data provided by each ealry intervention program in the state of Tennessee ($N = 176$). These self-report data were then weighted for importance by the scores provided by the panel of two hundred experts described earlier. A panel of twenty-one experts rated the profiles, and their results were compared to the predictions made from the original quality ranking of these programs. The results from the instrument accurately reflected the known quality of the setting. Judges reading about these components described those that had high-quality ratings as significantly more effective, comprehensive, and higher in quality.

In the third stage, an effectiveness study was conducted. Outcome measures were developed that included a form for parents and teachers to report their perceptions of the transition component in terms of the children's adjustments to the new setting and the appropriateness of the placement and the placement process. A total of twenty-two were selected, with eleven having high-quality transition components and eleven having low-quality components. Parents and teachers in the schools that received the children in the following year were asked to rate the children's behavior on a number of dimensions. The quality of the preschool's transition component significantly related to the teacher's rating on process and placement, but not on adjustment. Parents rated their children who had been served by high-quality transition components as being better adjusted to the new program and being more appropriately placed, but they did not discern differences in the placement process.

In terms of defining the contributive value of the transition components to the preschool program, statistical relationships were assessed between the component quality and the overall program quality. Our results indicated a strong positive relationship between component quality and project quality (Pearson correlation coefficient = .56). Although we cannot attribute project quality solely to a single component, it does indicate that good things tend to go together in preschool programs. Additionally, analysis of the data from these projects indicated that children coming from programs rated high in quality by the quality instrument were rated more positively in terms of their transition to their new setting by teachers and parents. Overall, then, we believe these results lend support to the validity of the CQC and the quality methodology.

Additional Applications of Quality Instrumentation

Quality measures can be used in various ways. First, quality measures can be used to provide program administrators and sponsors with descriptive and prescriptive feedback in an efficient manner. At a general level, a quality-assessment instrument can be used to determine what services were rendered and how they were provided. At the interpretive level, the instrument provides data about how well the program is functioning.

Second, because the quality measure is standardized, it allows communication between various agencies, departments, and work units in a program or between programs via a common language. Program descriptions can be circulated among administrators so that they can compare their program with others. Clearly, the best way to accomplish this may be to ensure some measure of anonymity. Increased communication between or within groups frequently leads to more resource exchange and improved service delivery. In this sense, quality measures have the potential to provide indirect program benefits.

Third, the use of standardized assessment instruments leads to comparable, aggregatable data that benefits the program area as a whole. By reporting the results of instruments used in different contexts in published papers, the field as a whole gains a better notion of how to improve program services. These data would also reflect on program theory. Because theory based on social science knowledge frequently requires updating and modification, the validation of theory-driven quality measures also validates aspects of that theory. In other words, failure to validate some measure of quality, in the absence of methodological flaws, indicates that the theory deserves reevaluation.

Fourth, quality assessment can substitute for impact studies (Bickman, 1989; Chen, 1989). Impact studies are expensive to conduct, leaving few resources for the development and testing of program theory. An alternative form of theory-driven evaluation is theory-based quality assessment. When there is substantial and consistent evidence of the predictive validity of the quality indicators, then impact studies should no longer be required because quality indicators can be used as performance measures with confidence that they actually relate to outcome.

The application of quality measures is not without problems. Findings rendered by the instrument may not be politically acceptable. Agencies or programs may not appreciate being compared to others, particularly when there are readily observable differences in service availability or funding. In this sense, the instrument's advantage of increasing communication can become a liability. However, such liabilities are frequently a part of evaluation, and overcoming them is part of the challenge of conducting evaluations.

Additionally, although we validated the instrument through the opinions of informed experts and the actual changes in program participants, certain questions are difficult to address. Specifically, the quality approach does not provide simple methods for direct comparisons of effectiveness between components. For example, we were not able to determine with this technology whether transition services were more effective than the family intervention component. To do so would have required cost-benefit analysis, where each component is costed and the comparisons are made on a dollar value basis.

Conclusion

Changes in the nature of evaluation have served to emphasize an understanding of how, and not simply whether, a program works. One key to addressing this question of how is deciding what stakeholders value in terms of process and outcome and then developing ways of measuring those phenomena. We propose that the notion of quality is an effective orienting device for assessing programs, and that to tap program quality we must begin with a clear idea of program theory. From theory the evaluator obtains a description of the program and a viewpoint about the innovations' valued outputs. Together, this descriptive and prescriptive information directs the measurement process, in terms of both choosing what to measure and selecting a method.

References

Berwick, D. M. "Continuous Improvement as an Ideal in Health Care." *New England Journal of Medicine,* 1989, *320,* 53–56.
Bickman, L. "Improving Established Statewide Programs: A Component Theory of Evaluation." *Evaluation Review,* 1985, *9,* 189–208.
Bickman, L. "Barriers to the Use of Program Theory." *Evaluation and Program Planning,* 1989, *12,* 387–390.
Brook, R., Davies, A. R., and Kamberg, C. J. "Selected Reflections on Quality of Medical Care Evaluation in the 1980s." *Nursing Research,* 1980, *29,* 127–132.
Brook, R., Kamberg, C. J., and Lohr, K. "Quality Assessment in Mental Health." *Professional Psychology,* 1983, *13,* 34–39.
Califano, J. A. *America's Health Care Revolution.* New York: Touchstone, 1986.
Chen, H.-T. "The Conceptual Framework of the Theory-Driven Perspective." *Evaluation and Program Planning,* 1989, *12,* 391–396.
Deming, W. E. *Quality, Productivity, and Competitive Position.* Cambridge: Massachusetts Institute of Technology, Center for Advanced Engineering Study, 1982.
Deming, W. E. *Out of the Crisis.* Cambridge: Massachusetts Institute of Technology, Center for Advanced Engineering Study, 1986.
Dewey, J. *Experience and Education.* New York: Macmillan, 1938.
Donabedian, A. "Evaluating Quality of Care." *Milbank Memorial Fund Quarterly,* 1966, *44,* 166–206.

Donabedian, A. "Explorations in Quality Assessment and Monitoring." In *The Definition of Quality and Approaches to Its Assessment.* Vol 1. Ann Arbor, Mich.: Health Administration Press, 1980.

Juran, J. M. *Managerial Breakthrough.* New York: McGraw-Hill, 1964.

Juran, J. M., Gryna, F. M., Jr., and Bingham, R. S., Jr. (eds.). *Quality Control Handbook.* New York: McGraw-Hill, 1979.

Lipsey, M. W., Crosse, S., Dunkle, J., Pollard, J., and Stobart, G. "Evaluation: The State of the Art and the Sorry State of the Science." *New Directions for Program Evaluation,* 1985, *27,* 7–28.

Nichols, J. G. *The Competitive Ethos and Democratic Education.* Cambridge, Mass.: Harvard University Press, 1989.

Pirsig, R. M. *Zen and the Art of Motorcycle Maintenance: An Inquiry into Values.* New York: Bantam Books, 1974.

Vuori, H. "Optimal and Logical Quality: Two Neglected Aspects of the Quality of Health Services." *Medical Care,* 1980, *18,* 975–985.

Leonard Bickman is a professor of psychology at Peabody College, Vanderbilt University, and director of the Center for Mental Health Policy at the Vanderbilt Institute for Public Policy Studies, Nashville, Tennessee.

Keith A. Peterson is a research associate at the Social Ecology Laboratory, Veterans Administration Medical Center, Palo Alto, California.

Methods used and lessons learned in developing and testing theories about the nature and functioning of adult day care are described.

Developing and Testing Program Classification and Function Theories

Kendon J. Conrad, Janet R. Buelow

Evaluation theorists have been increasingly concerned with program theory (Chen and Rossi, 1983, 1989; Bickman, 1987; 1989). While this movement has clarified many important principles, definitions, and methods, there continues to be a low level of theorizing in the actual practice of program evaluation (Chen and Rossi, 1989; Lipsey and Pollard, 1989). In recent projects designed to evaluate adult day care (ADC), we have been building the capability to develop and test theories about the nature and functioning of ADC. The purpose of this chapter is to share some of our practical experience in this effort. Specifically, we present examples from a series of developmental studies that led to the testing of program theories. These studies involve (1) obtaining thorough substantive and experiential knowledge of the program, (2) describing the program by obtaining detailed information on a large sample of projects, (3) developing the ability to measure program characteristics reliably and validly from the perspective of major program stakeholders, (4) developing and testing theories about the various classes of projects that exist within a program, and (5) developing and testing theories about how the program

---

The research reported in this chapter was supported by funds from the Retirement Research Foundation, the American Association of Retired Persons Andrus Foundation, and the Department of Veterans Affairs. We are grateful to Karen M. Conrad and Leonard Bickman for suggestions on an earlier draft and to Jeffery Parker for manuscript assistance.

and/or classes of the program function to affect outcomes. We then discuss how these theory-driven studies can contribute to improved program evaluation and policy analysis.

Definitions

In an earlier paper (Conrad and Miller, 1987), we described the elements of a "philosophy-testing evaluation." The word *philosophy* was used instead of *theory* to emphasize the fact that theories alone do not determine program characteristics. Values underlie the choice of theories, and therefore they influence structure, process, and outcome. We referred to the convergence of theories and values as philosophy. Another important definition that we employed was the distinction between *program* and *project* (Cook, Leviton, and Shadish, 1985). Program is the genre or species of service such as the ADC program (Conrad, Hughes, Campione, and Goldberg, 1987), the child-parent center program (Conrad and Eash, 1983), and the Head Start Program (Westinghouse Learning Corporation, 1969). Projects are the local centers that actually deliver the services to a particular set of clients in a particular setting, for example, the Bright Side Adult Day Care Center in Rockford, Illinois, the Hansberry Child Parent Center in Chicago, and the Lawndale Head Start project in Chicago.

When planners design a project, they do not usually compose a program theory; rather, they write a mission statement, a rationale, or a philosophy designed to guide the implementation of the project at a particular site for particular clients. Therefore, philosophy is particular to the project. It follows that if there are fifteen hundred ADC centers in the United States, there are fifteen hundred different philosophies. These philosophies will probably have some core similarities, but they will also have great differences. We have learned that we cannot do a good job of evaluating a program if we do not take these project differences into account (Cook, Leviton, and Shadish, 1985).

Theorizing is involved in planning new programs. These theories are usually prescriptive (Chen, this volume) and state what the program should accomplish and how this should be done. However, because of the necessary compromise involved in getting these programs funded, these theories are, of necessity, kept general and vague (Pressman and Wildavsky, 1973). Additionally, it is not possible to anticipate, before implementation, all of the various adaptations that a program will undergo to fit the infinite variety of situations in which it will be attempted (Roberts-Gray and Scheirer, 1988). There is a vast gulf between the "should be" of early theory and the "is" of an actual program. The gulf is also great between early prescriptive theories and the testing of whether those theories actually work.

When programs are new, the values and theories (that is, philosophy) involved in their planning should be clearly explicated, measured, and tested at the project level (Conrad and Miller, 1987). This can reduce the disparity between intention and implementation. When several projects have been implemented, the empirical development and testing of program theories are possible. Based on experience derived from program implementation, these theories can go far beyond initial, usually naive, statements. They can become quite credible and detailed and thus contribute to improved practice.

A program theorist measures the characteristics of the projects of a program, clarifies them, and composes sets of statements about how the program as a whole and how various individual classes work to achieve their respective outcomes. Therefore, program theories involve the aggregation of projects and may include all projects or classes of projects.

Measuring Program Characteristics

The ability to measure program characteristics is essential to developing, testing, and refining program theory (Conrad and Hughes, 1989; Conrad and Miller, 1987; Moos, 1974; Nunnally, 1978). Unfortunately, standardized valid measures of theoretically relevant program characteristics are rare (Bickman, 1989). We recognized this when we became involved in studying ADC, a relatively new and rapidly expanding day program for frail and functionally impaired adults (Conrad, Hanrahan, and Hughes, 1990).

Content Knowledge. Since we recognized the importance of measurement, our first project was to develop instruments useful in measuring the program environments of ADC and their structures, processes, and populations. To do so required obtaining a close familiarity with the content area, getting a good idea of what ADC is and how it works through one's own experience and the experience of others (Bickman, 1989). This was done under a subcontract from the Adult Day Health Care Evaluation of the Department of Veterans Affairs (VA) (Hedrick, Inui, Rothman, and Watts, 1984). The project attempted to draw upon existing measures, but the only one with clear application was the Multiphasic Environmental Assessment Procedure (Moos and Lemke, 1984). To get a clearer understanding of the issues involved, we visited several ADC centers, composed pilot measures, field-tested them, and had them reviewed by the VA advisory committee of ADC providers, researchers, and policymakers, who addressed issues of content, coverage, and face validity of the measures. The project resulted in a set of measures we called the Adult Day Care Assessment Procedure (ADCAP).

Describing the Program. Since ADC was a relatively new program, an obvious use for these new measures was the description of its characteristics. With funding from the American Association of Retired Persons Andrus Foundation, we conducted a national census survey of ADC centers in the United States. The ADCAP was sent to the on-site directors of the 1,373

ADC centers in the directory of the National Institute of Adult Daycare. The response was 974 usable questionnaires, or 72.3 percent of eligible respondents. This data base was useful in getting a general idea of the nature of ADC in terms of its structure, activities and services, and client population across the United States and within the four U.S. census regions (Conrad and Roberts-Gray, 1988). This basic description was important in refining questions about how ADC works (that is, in developing theory) because it confirmed the existing lore about great variation in what ADC is. The implication is that one theory would be too general to have strong, clear, practical application.

Metric Properties. The survey data base also provided the opportunity to analyze the metric properties of the ADCAP instruments. Items were studied for their distributional characteristics. Factor analysis was used to assist the development of scales and subscales (that is, to confirm, deny, and inform the a priori specification). Internal consistency estimates (Cronbach, 1951) were obtained for the resulting refined scales (Conrad and Hughes, 1989). In a subsequent study funded by the Retirement Research Foundation, test-retest reliability estimates were obtained.

Multiple Stakeholders. With the ADCAP census survey, we had obtained all of the data from on-site administrators of the ADC centers. However, we recognized that other parties have just as great a stake in these centers—other staff, clients, and the home caregivers of the clients. While the importance of ADC to the administrators, staff, and clients seems obvious, ADC is also important to the home caregivers because it provides respite from the continuous burden of caring for a disabled family member. It may also enable the home caregiver to maintain the relative at home while continuing gainful employment.

Each of these stakeholders has a valid, but different, perspective on the ADC center. These varying perspectives had to be taken into account if our measures of project characteristics were to be considered valid. Figure 1 presents the ADC characteristics measured for each of the four project stakeholders.

As the fifth type of stakeholder we regard all those who are not necessarily involved with a project first-hand. They are not providers or recipients but instead are concerned with the effects of the program as a whole on society. Although this disparate array could be subdivided in other contexts, we include the policymaker, the funding source, the program evaluator, the media, and the taxpayer for the purpose of this chapter. This stakeholder, as represented by these various types of professions, funds the program, commissions the evaluation, collects data, analyzes them, and reports on the program's quality and effectiveness. The existence of a fifth stakeholder implies the need to measure this party's perception of ADC. Although we recognize this need, our measurement of it is rudimentary at this time and, therefore, is not described here.

Figure 1. The Adult Day Care Assessment Procedure (ADCAP)

Administrators and Staff			Clients

Program Structure Sections

Structural Features	Policy and Program Information	Staffing Sections	Structure
			Window-areas
Location	Linkages with	Volunteers and	Level of lighting
Space and	other organi-	students	General attractiveness
facilities	zations	Core and	
Bathrooms and	Program auspices	consulting staff	**Social Environment**
toilets	Staff training	Administrator	Communication
Equipment/	Funding sources		Staff caring
furniture			Morale problems
Activity areas			
Transportation			**Services and Activities**
			Health services
			Rehabilitation
			Social-recreational
			Counseling

Care Process Sections

Social Environment Scales	Services and Activities	Outcome
		Client satisfaction
General morale	Clinic services	
Staff cooperation	Case management	*Home Caregivers*
Independence-promoting	Activities of daily living	
approach	Counseling	**Structure**
Communication	Play	Convenience
Caring/extroversion	Respite	Pleasant environment
Director control	Therapeutic recreation	
Social involvement	Physical therapy	**Social Environment**
Isolation/introversion	Prescription and diet	Morale problems
Team organization	Client education	Care process
	Family education	Communication
	Group support	
	Planning with family	**Services and Activities**
	Religious services	Client activities
		Client services
		Counseling
		Family support
		Outings
		Personal enrichment

Population Selection

Client description (ADL, IADL, diagnosis)
Discharge information

Outcome
General strain
Time spent in
  caregiving
Expense

Theory Development and Testing: A General Strategy

As Lipsey and Pollard (1989) have pointed out, it is hard to imagine an area in which some sort of relevant concepts, research, or theory have not been developed by academicians, policymakers, or practitioners. These ideas can be articulated in the form of theoretical expectations about the nature of the existing classes of the project and about the functioning of the program both within and across classes.

In several different ways, we have employed a general strategy called "pattern matching" to test theoretical expectations against our empirical findings. Trochim (1989) and his colleagues have described and demonstrated the theory of pattern matching in program evaluation (Marquart, this volume). Pattern matching always involves an attempt to link two patterns, where one is a theoretical pattern and the other is an observed or operational pattern. In the theoretical realm, existing theories, research studies, and the ideas and hunches of stakeholders are formulated as a coherent pattern, the theory. In evaluation, Wholey (1979, 1987) has characterized a method for formulating the theoretical pattern that he calls "logic modeling." Path analysis or structural equation modeling is another general method of articulating the theoretical pattern that involves detailed specification of the operationalization, measurement, and relationships of the variables in the theory (Jöreskog and Sörbom, 1984; Smith, this volume).

In the observational realm, data are collected and analyzed, and the resulting patterns are observed and matched with the theoretical pattern. The extent of the fit or match between the patterns serves to support or refute the theory and usually leads to rethinking or adjustment of the theory in some way (Trochim 1989). Throughout the remainder of this chapter, examples are provided of the use of pattern matching in testing theory against observations.

Program Classification Theories

Within any program, there is variation in mission and philosophy with a corresponding variation in other characteristics. In other words, projects vary in practice. As a result, a general program theory may not be specific enough to enable a clear understanding of various types of projects. One aspect of program theory involves classification of projects in terms of their philosophies, structures, processes, and outcomes. This classification of the projects can be made in at least three general ways based on (1) policy relevance of the classes, (2) relevance to practice and treatment issues, and (3) theoretical expectations and observations regarding the similarities of the centers on key characteristics.

Policy-Relevant Classification. Policymakers may be interested in classifying programs according to characteristics that influence funding levels, target populations, and so forth. In ADC, for example, such policy-relevant classification is important in clarifying the characteristics of urban versus rural centers. This is because approximately 30 percent of the elderly live in rural areas and the proportion of rural elderly is growing faster than the urban counterpart. This pattern of growth, along with a lack of development of rural long-term care systems, raises the policy issue of the relative health service disadvantage of the rural elderly. This issue is being addressed with the ADCAP census data base by examining urban centers, defined as those in Standard Metropolitan Statistical Areas (SMSAs) versus those not in SMSAs (rural).

Another important policy issue is Medicare funding for ADC. Adult day care services are not currently reimbursable under Medicare as are nursing home and home health services. To become Medicare supported, ADC centers must show that they play a necessary role in maintaining the health of their clients. Policymakers need information to define a health-oriented model of ADC. With the ADCAP data base, we can classify centers according to a variety of relevant characteristics such as client population, service provision, staffing, and equipment. Criteria for all of these components can be measured and used in clarifying the characteristics of and addressing the important issue of funding for Medicare-model ADC.

Practice-Relevant Classification. Service providers are interested in classifying programs according to the characteristics of special subpopulations and corresponding service characteristics. For example, ADC centers have recently opened that serve client populations consisting entirely or predominantly of victims of Alzheimer's disease and similar chronic dementias. Theoretically, these centers should differ from centers not serving the cognitively impaired as the principal clientele.

We are using the ADCAP data base to clarify the theory of care for Alzheimer's disease victims in ADC. To do so, we have stated our theoretical expectations for Alzheimer's-type ADC centers (having more that 30 percent Alzheimer's clients) versus the rest of the centers and tested whether these expectations were, in fact, supported by the data. If they were, theory and practice would be consistent, and we would be reassured that (1) we understand how ADC is being provided and (2) that it is being provided as it should be. If our expectations and our findings were not consistent, we would ask (1) is the theory wrong or (2) should practice be changed to become more consistent with theory? We close this section with a description of a part of this study of Alzheimer's-type ADC and a discussion of some applications to practice.

The criterion for defining a program as one primarily geared for victims of Alzheimer's disease (ALZ) was that 30 percent or more of clients had ALZ. An estimate of this percentage was obtained from each center administrator. The rationale for choosing centers having 30 percent or more clients with ALZ was that the proportion of these clients was so great that the characteristics of the center would necessarily be affected in order to address their special needs (Chodosh, Zeffert, and Muro, 1986).

To provide a comparison by which to assess the characteristics of centers treating ALZ, we chose those centers having less that 30 percent Alzheimer's clients (non-ALZ). This group of centers would probably serve a variety of populations, from the relatively unimpaired to alert clients having severe physical impairments, but they would not be especially adapted to meet the needs of clients with ALZ. After the a priori grouping, we found that the actual average percentage of clients with Alzheimer's disease in ALZ centers was 51.3 percent and in non-ALZ 8.7 percent.

Regarding the characteristics of the social environment, we expected the ALZ centers would tend to have more morale problems because of difficulties involved in care of ALZ victims; there would be less of an independence-promoting approach because of the irreversible nature of the disease, less communication because of the difficulties involved in communicating with ALZ victims, more caring and extroverted behavior on the part of staff, and more social involvement. We did not expect any differences in regard to staff cooperation with each other or in the amount of director control exercised.

The Social Environment scales consisted of the administrators' ratings of seven characteristics of the social environment of the centers on four response categories: 1 = strongly disagree, 2 = disagree, 3 = agree, and 4 = strongly agree. Morale Problems indicated problems in morale, primarily in clients (clients complain, start arguments). Staff Cooperation assessed the degree to which staff were perceived as having good working relations (staff work well together, staff work as a team). Independence-Promoting Approach assessed the degree to which clients initiated or were encouraged to initiate activities (clients learn to do things on their own, clients not able to do much). Communication indicated the degree to which client-staff interaction was perceived as warm and attentive (staff spend time with clients, clients get individual attention). Director Control measured degree of centralization of authority in the hands of the director (director affects promotion of subordinates, information is shared freely among staff). Caring/Extroversion assessed the manner of treatment and level of attention given by the staff to clients. Social Involvement measured importance placed on involvement of family and community (important to involve family, ADC has program to change community attitudes toward the aged).

Our theoretical expectations regarding differences between ALZ and non-ALZ centers on the characteristics of interest were tested using two-tailed t-tests. The theoretical expectations were stated as "+" (ALZ centers would score higher), "ns" (no significant differences between the two groups), and "–" (ALZ centers would score lower). The results are presented in Table 1.

Table 1. Expectations and *t*-Tests of Differences Between
Alzheimer's (ALZ) and Non-Alzheimer's (Non-ALZ)
Models of Adult Day Care on Process Measures

Scale Item	Group	N	Expectation	t-Value
Morale problems	ALZ	229	+	-3.64[a]
	Non-ALZ	541		
Staff cooperation	ALZ	239	ns	-.06
	Non-ALZ	568		
Independence-promoting approach	ALZ	232	-	-3.66[a]
	Non-ALZ	558		
Communication	ALZ	234	-	1.54
	Non-ALZ	570		
Director control	ALZ	227	ns	2.07
	Non-ALZ	553		
Caring/extroversion	ALZ	236	+	3.13[a]
	Non-ALZ	565		
Social involvement	ALZ	238	+	4.52[a]
	Non-ALZ	557		

[a] $p \leq .001$.

In five out of seven cases our findings were consistent with our expectations. There was no difference in Staff Cooperation or Director Control. As expected, the use of an Independence-Promoting Approach to care was significantly lower in ALZ centers, whereas Caring/Extroversion and Social Involvement were higher. We had hypothesized that Communication would be lower in ALZ centers because of the difficulties ALZ clients have in this area, but we found no such difference. The most counterintuitive finding was that ALZ centers reported fewer Morale Problems that non-ALZ centers. Because of the severity of Alzheimer's disease and the consequent problems in dealing with its victims, we had expected more morale problems in the ALZ centers. Such a counterintuitive finding deserves further exploration and a reconsideration of expectations. We need to replicate this finding and explain it.

Theoretical/Observational Classification. Although it is impossible to disregard a priori notions such as those mentioned previously in classifying projects, it is important from a social science perspective to develop an objective classification system that is consistent with observations of the natural variation within a program, for example, classifying centers based on the observed commonality of their characteristics without preliminary regard to policy considerations or practical/clinical applications. Once again, we believe it is important to state any existing expectations first, collect observations, and classify projects based on the observed relationships among the projects on key variables. We present two examples of how one might accomplish this below.

An Early Survey of ADC. The earliest survey and description of ADC in the United States attempted to describe various models among the eighteen centers existing at that time (Weissert, 1977). Although it did not have a preconceived pattern of expectations, Weissert's survey of ten centers did derive two models form observations made through visiting the centers: model 1 was predominantly rehabilitation-oriented and model 2 was multipurpose, though usually less health-oriented. Model 1 centers tended to be targeted toward a specific, posthospital, rehabilitation-needing client group with many limitations in activities of daily living. Model 2 centers admitted clients who were older, needed fewer health services, had less impairment, and often came to ADC before going to a nursing home rather than after an institutional stay.

Although Weissert's sample was small, it was important because it demonstrated that ADC can fill a variety of roles and that centers can specialize or target their services to a particular clientele. Since the early 1970s, ADC centers have proliferated dramatically. From eighteen centers in 1974, the number has increased to seventeen hundred as estimated by the National Institute on Adult Daycare (Von Behren, 1988). With the growth of ADC, it is possible to test theory about program classes using empirical estimation procedures, as we describe below.

Refining Models of ADC: A Cluster Analysis. As pressure increases to find less expensive and less restrictive alternatives to hospitals and nursing homes, policymakers will look to ADC to accommodate a more severely impaired clientele. As our population ages, ADC will be called on to provide a plethora of community-based services to clients and their home caregivers in order to promote healthy aging and prevent avoidable institutionalization. Therefore, it seems likely to us that ADC centers will differ substantially, depending on their chosen purposes, the characteristics of their client populations, and the characteristics of their communities.

For example, in urban areas with a dense population having large numbers of elderly and a comprehensive network of service linkages, it would be quite feasible and appropriate for a center to focus on heavy-care versus light-care clients or on a specialized population such as ALZ victims. In suburban or rural areas where the elderly population is sparse, we expect that centers will be forced to meet a wide spectrum of needs and will take on a multipurpose character. Of course, it will also be convenient to have multipurpose centers in urban areas. However, since centers tend to be small, averaging about twenty clients per day (Conrad, Hanrahan, and Hughes, 1990), it is likely that many centers will specialize whenever possible, for much the same reason that nursing homes now group residents into intermediate, skilled, confused, or special-care categories.

The ability to describe classes has several important implications for improved practice. For example, a description of the characteristics of centers serving a heavy-care population would be useful to those serving this population insofar as they could compare themselves to the norm, compare the norm to their ideal, and draw conclusions about areas needing improvement both for their own particular centers and for centers in general. Such descriptions would be useful to neophytes by providing rough guidelines for common practice in the start-up of new centers. As noted earlier, the ability to describe the characteristics of a Medicare-fundable model of ADC will also enable policymakers to set criteria for funding and would give providers clear guidelines for attaining eligibility.

The spokespersons for ADC have officially disavowed the idea that different models or classes of ADC exist. The National Institute of Adult Daycare prefers the generic term *adult day care* for all types of day programs and states that "although funding and licensing may have roughly shaped a health and social model, where one provides health services such as nursing and the other does not, our perception is that over the years the lines of demarcation have blurred" (Von Behren, 1988, p. 3).

We do not believe that this conclusion is warranted without further empirical evidence. In a proposed project, we would regard the existence of distinguishable classes as an open question. The analysis of the 1986 ADCAP data base revealed great variation in the characteristic of ADC (Conrad, Hanrahan, and Hughes, 1990). The proposed analysis would explain that variation more completely. Our current thought is that centers would be likely to cluster into four groups: heavy care (requiring medical and rehabilitative services), light care (focusing on social needs), multipurpose (providing a complete spectrum of services and activities), and specialized (serving a subpopulation such as clients requiring rehabilitation and victims of Alzheimer's or Parkinson's disease).

We are using a clustering algorithm to group centers according to the commonality or their services and activities. Our methods are proceeding as follows:

1. Definition of a set of variables on which to measure the characteristics of ADC (that is, the ADCAP)
2. Collection of data on a large sample of centers in the national survey
3. Data reduction using factor analysis
4. Choice of a theoretically relevant set of variables to use in clustering centers
5. Cluster analysis using the SPSS^x clustering program
6. Description or profiling of the groups using the full set of variables.

Having accomplished the theoretical development and testing of classes, we are ready to examine the ways in which the classes function to affect client outcomes.

Program Function Theories

A program function theory is a set of statements describing how program characteristics (that is, structure and process) affect client outcomes. After classification of projects, program function theory is useful in clarifying how a program accomplishes its effects both within and across the classes of the program. To illustrate the methods we have used in developing and testing function theories of ADC, a part of an ADCAP study that is currently in progress is described below.

How ADC Structure and Process Affect Outcomes. In a follow-up to the national survey funded by the Retirement Research Foundation, we were interested in determining the major factors that influenced clients' satisfaction with ADC. Unfortunately, we could not find solid theories on this topic. Most studies were qualitative, which makes them difficult to replicate. The quantitative studies tended to focus on structural features that were relatively easy to measure while neglecting social processes of care. A review of program components and their effect on general satisfaction in ADC and in health care settings in general revealed that both structure and process components were associated with client satisfaction.

Using data collected from seventy-four ADC centers, this study measured the characteristics of ADC as perceived by 238 clients (see Table 2). Our theory stated that client general satisfaction with ADC is significantly associated with client perception of staff caring, general morale, communication, interior structure of the center, and availability of services (see Figure 2).

We tested this theory first by estimating the correlations of the clients' perceptions of program characteristics and their general satisfaction with the program (Table 2). Six of the eight program components were significantly correlated with general satisfaction. Communication and health services were the two variables not significantly correlated with client general satisfaction. The most strongly correlated variables with general satisfaction were staff caring, general morale, and interior structure. Their correlation coefficients were .56, .42, and .40, respectively ($p \leq .001$). Three service variables—rehabilitation services, social-recreational services, and counseling services—had moderate but significant ($p \leq .05$) correlations with general satisfaction levels. Their correlation coefficients were .27, .16, and .14, respectively.

These effects of the program components were then examined using general linear regression. General satisfaction was regressed on the eight program components, as perceived by clients. With this model, 43 percent of the variance in general satisfaction was accounted for ($p \leq .01$). However, only three of the eight program components were found to contribute significantly to the model (see Mark, this volume, for the "purification approach"). These variables were staff caring, general morale, and interior

Table 2. Measures of ADC Program Characteristics and Client Satisfaction

Program Components and Alpha-Reliability Values		Sample of Scale Items
A.	Staff caring alpha = .706	A-1	Information about the program is shared freely
		A-2	When clients ask staff for help, their requests are usually taken care of right away
B.	General morale alpha = .740	B-1	Clients complain a lot
		B-2	Clients sometimes start arguments
C.	Communication alpha = .725	C-1	Clients talk about their many problems
		C-2	Clients openly talk about their personal problems
D.	Interior structure alpha = .587	D-1	Window areas in main activity rooms
		D-2	Level of lighting in main activity rooms
E.	Health services alpha = .749	E-1	Optometry services
		E-2	Hearing examinations
F.	Rehabilitation services alpha = .755	F-1	Physical therapy
		F-2	Speech therapy
G.	Social-Recreational alpha = .711	G-1	Arts and crafts
		G-2	Parties
H.	Counseling services alpha = .700	H-1	Individual counseling
		H-2	Group counseling
GS.	General satisfaction (dependent variable) alpha = .779	GS-1	Coming to the center makes client feel good
		GS-2	There are some things about the care that could be better

Note: For an explanation of the alpha-reliability statistic, see Cronbach, 1951.

**Figure 2. Client Perceptions of ADC Characteristics
and Their General Satisfaction: Original Model**

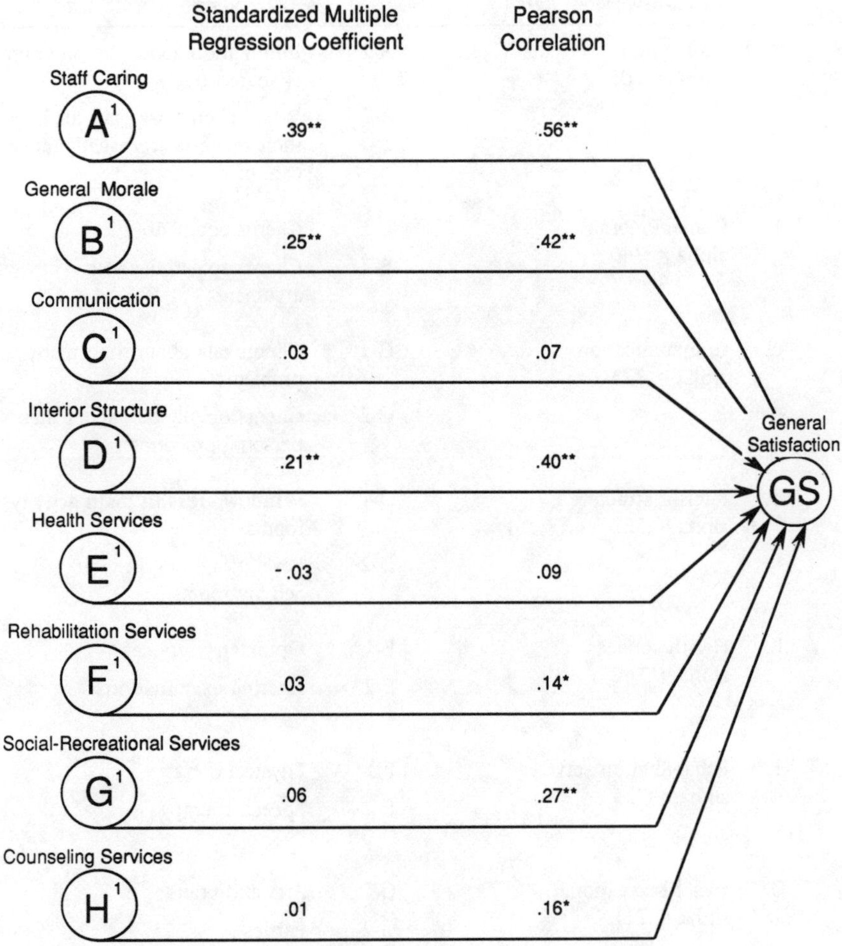

	Standardized Multiple Regression Coefficient	Pearson Correlation
Staff Caring — A[1]	.39**	.56**
General Morale — B[1]	.25**	.42**
Communication — C[1]	.03	.07
Interior Structure — D[1]	.21**	.40**
Health Services — E[1]	-.03	.09
Rehabilitation Services — F[1]	.03	.14*
Social-Recreational Services — G[1]	.06	.27**
Counseling Services — H[1]	.01	.16*

General Satisfaction — GS

Note: R^2 = .43 ($p \leq .01$), N = 228.
*$p \leq .05$
**$p \leq .01$

structure with standardized regression coefficients of .39, .25. and .21, respectively (Figure 2). When the nonsignificant variables were dropped from the model, the R^2 remained fundamentally the same, indicating that clients' perceptions of services were mediated by their perceptions of staff caring, general morale, and interior structure (see Figure 3).

Significance of This Modest Theory. The foregoing development and testing of a theory about how a program affects client satisfaction is important to evaluators because it represents an attempt to verify the "active causal ingredients" of a program. Although this is only part of a study, even this modest example has practical applications for the marketing of and quality assurance in ADC (Cleary and McNeal, 1988; Ware and Davies, 1983). From the marketing perspective, the consequences of dissatisfied clients may be the discontinuation of service usage. Therefore, successful marketing of services depends on the ability of the provider to maximize client satisfaction. Our theory gives some direction useful in accomplishing this objective.

From the perspective of quality assurance, client satisfaction plays an essential role in assessing the quality of care provided to a client. Many quality assurance experts today support the theory that client satisfaction is one desired outcome for health care services; and if clients ar satisfied, then the services provided must have met a minimum degree of quality (Donabedian, 1980; Davies and Ware, 1988; Vuori, 1982).

Specifically, it was found that the three most important program components affecting client satisfaction were staff caring, general morale, and

Figure 3. Client Perceptions of ADC Characteristics and Their General Satisfaction: Refined Model

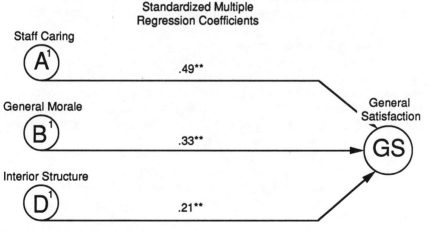

Standardized Multiple
Regression Coefficients

Staff Caring

(A¹)

.49**

General Morale

(B¹)

.33**

General
Satisfaction

(GS)

Interior Structure

(D¹)

.21**

Note: $R^2 = .42$ ($p \leq .01$), $N = 228$.
**$p \leq .01$

interior structure of the center. Clearly, if these components affect client satisfaction, they are important quality indicators too. It follows that these program components represent areas that should be emphasized when marketing ADC centers and assessing their quality (Bickman, this volume).

These findings are consistent with the results of previous research and indicate to practitioners, administrators, and program reviewers where to focus their attention when seeking to improve service delivery and utilization. This study is important to researchers insofar as it employs quantitative methodology in assessing important aspects of programs that have usually been treated with qualitative methods. In particular, this study had a large enough sample of ADC centers to enable inferences at the intended level of analysis, the center (Whiting-O'Keefe, Henke, and Simborg, 1984; Koepke and Flay, 1989). Additionally, it provides a beginning in measurement and analysis that enable and encourage replication and falsification (Popper, 1972; Cook and Campbell, 1979).

Implications for Evaluation Practice

Once again a key issue for the practice of program evaluation is the distinction between project and program. It is not appropriate to disregard the single project evaluation in the effort to develop program theories across projects. To have successful programs, it is crucial for evaluation to assess philosophy, structure, population, process, and outcome (Conrad and Miller, 1987) at the project level. These assessments provide a feedback mechanism that enables improvement of the project. Comprehensive assessment procedures like the ADCAP can facilitate these project assessments by providing quantitative descriptions form multiple perspectives. They can also be used to aggregate data across projects to develop and test program theories.

This chapter demonstrated a way to achieve detailed and relatively comprehensive measurements of the characteristics of a large sample of projects within a program. It discussed strategies for developing and testing theories about the classes of projects within a program (see Cronkite and Moos, 1980; Moos and Lemke, 1984). Finally, it presented an approach to developing and testing theories of how the classes of a program function to promote improved client outcomes.

A major advantage of this general approach to program evaluation is that it provides a set of standardized measures of a program's characteristics that can be used by anyone interested in studying a program, a class of a program, or a particular project (Moos, 1988). Eventually, this approach can facilitate replication of findings and can serve as a heuristic device and a catalyst for the development and testing of empirically based theories of how programs in general work.

References

Bickman, L. (ed.). *Using Program Theory in Evaluation*. New Directions for Program Evaluation, no. 33. San Francisco: Jossey-Bass, 1987.

Bickman, L. "Barriers to the Use of Program Theory." *Evaluation and Program Planning*, 1989, *12*, 387-390.

Chen, H.-T., and Rossi, P. H. "Evaluating with Sense: The Theory-Driven Approach." *Evaluation Review*, 1983, *7*, 283-302.

Chen, H.-T., and Rossi, P. H. "Issues in the Theory-Driven Perspective." *Evaluation and Program Planning*, 1989, *12*, 299-306.

Chodosh, H. L., Zeffert, B., and Muro, E. S. "Treatment of Dementia in a Medical Day Care Program." *Journal of American Geriatric Society*, 1986, *34*, 881-886.

Cleary, P. D., and McNeal, B. J. "Patient Satisfaction as an Indicator of Quality Care." *Inquiry*, 1988, *25*, 25-36.

Conrad, K. J., and Eash, M. J. "Measuring Implementation and Multiple Outcomes in a Child-Parent Center Compensatory Education Program." *American Educational Research Journal*, 1983, *20*, 221-236.

Conrad, K. J., Hanrahan, P., and Hughes, S. L. "Survey of Adult Day Care in the U.S.: National and Regional Findings." *Research on Aging*, 1990, *12*, 35-56.

Conrad, K. J., and Hughes, S. L. *Adult Day Care Assessment Procedure: Research Manual*. Working Paper No. 179. Evanston, Ill.: Center for Health Services and Policy Research, Northwestern University, 1989.

Conrad, K. J., Hughes, S. L., Campione, P. F., and Goldberg, R. S. "Shedding New Light on Adult Day Care." *Perspective on Aging*, 1987, *16*, 18-21.

Conrad, K. J., and Miller, T. Q. "Measuring and Testing Program Philosophy." In L. Bickman (ed.), *Using Program Theory in Evaluation*. New Directions for Program Evaluation. no. 33. San Francisco: Jossey-Bass, 1987.

Conrad, K. J., and Roberts-Gray, C. (eds.). *Evaluating Program Environments*. New Directions for Program Evaluation, no. 40. San Francisco: Jossey-Bass, 1988.

Cook, T. D., and Campbell, D. T. *Quasi-Experimentation: Design and Analysis Issues for Field Settings*. Skokie, Ill.: Rand McNally, 1979.

Cook, T. D., Leviton, L. C., and Shadish, W. R., Jr. "Program Evaluation." In G. Lindzey and E. Aronson (eds.), *The Handbook of Social Psychology*. (3rd ed.) New York: Random House, 1985.

Cronbach, L. J. "Coefficient Alpha and the Internal Structure of Tests." *Psychometrica*, 1951, *16*, 297-334.

Cronkite, R. C., and Moos, R. H. "Determinants of the Posttreatment Functioning of Alcoholic Patients: A Conceptual Framework." *Journal of Consulting and Clinical Psychology*, 1980, *48*, 305-316.

Davies, A., and Ware, J. "Involving Consumers in Quality of Care Assessment." *Health Affairs*, 1988, *7*, 33-48.

Donabedian, A. *The Definition of Quality and Approaches to Its Assessment. Explorations in Quality Assessment and Monitoring*. Vol 1. Ann Arbor, Mich.: Health Administration Press, 1980.

Hedrick S. C., Inui, T. S., Rothman, M. L., and Watts, C. A. "Evaluation of Effectiveness and Cost of Adult Day Health Care." Proposal funded by Veterans Administration Health Services Research and Development Service to HSR&D Field Program, American Lake Veterans Administration Medical Center, Tacoma, Washington, 1984.

Jöreskog, K. G., and Sörbom, D. *LISREL VI: Analysis of Linear Structural Relationships by Maximum Likelihood, Instrumental Variables, and Least-Squares Methods*. Mooresville, Ind.: Scientific Software, 1984.

Koepke, D., and Flay, B. "Levels of Analysis." In M. T. Braverman (ed.), *Evaluating Health Promotion Programs*. New Directions for Program Evaluation, no. 43. San Francisco: Jossey-Bass, 1989.

Lipsey, M., and Pollard, J. "Driving Toward Theory in Program Evaluation: More Models to Choose from." *Evaluation and Program Planning*, 1989, *12*, 317–328.

Moos, R. H. *Evaluating Treatment Environments: A Social Ecological Approach*. New York: Wiley, 1974.

Moos, R. H. "Assessing the Program Environment: Implications for Program Evaluation and Design." In K. J. Conrad and C. Roberts-Gray (eds.), *Evaluating Program Environments*. New Directions for Program Evaluation, no. 40. San Francisco: Jossey-Bass, 1988.

Moos, R. H., and Lemke, S. *Multiphasic Environmental Assessment Procedure (MEAP)*. Stanford, Calif.: Palo Alto Social Ecology Laboratory, Veterans Administration Medical Center, Stanford University, 1984.

Nunnally, J. C. *Psychometric Theory*. New York: McGraw-Hill, 1978.

Popper, K. R. *Objective Knowledge: An Evolutionary Approach*. Oxford, England: Clarendon Press, 1972.

Pressman, J. L., and Wildavsky, A. B. *Implementation*. Berkeley and Los Angeles: University of California Press, 1973.

Roberts-Gray, C., and Scheirer, M. A. "Checking the Congruence Between a Program and Its Organizational Environment." In K. J. Conrad and C. Roberts-Gray (eds.), *Evaluating Program Environments*. New Directions for Program Evaluation, no. 40. San Francisco: Jossey-Bass, 1988.

Trochim, W.M.K. "Outcome Pattern Matching and Program Theory." *Evaluation and Program Planning*, 1989, *12*, 355–366.

Von Behren, R. *Adult Day Care: A Program of Services for the Functionally Impaired*. Washington, D.C.: National Council on the Aging, National Institute of Adult Daycare, 1988.

Vuori, H. *Quality Assurance of Health Services: Concepts and Methodology*. Public Health in Europe No. 16. Copenhagen: World Health Organization, 1982.

Ware, J. E., and Davies, A. R. "Behavioral Consequences of Consumer Dissatisfaction with Medical Care." *Evaluation and Program Planning*, 1983, *6*, 29–297.

Weissert, W. G. "Adult Day Care in the United States. Current Research Projects and a Survey of Ten Centers." *Public Health Reports*, 1977, *92*, 49–56.

Westinghouse Learning Corporation/Ohio University. *The Impact of Head Start: An Evaluation of the Effects of Head Start on Children's Cognitive and Affective Development*. Washington, D.C.: Office of Economic Opportunity, 1969.

Whiting-O'Keefe, Q. E., Henke, C., and Simborg, D. W. "Choosing the Correct Unit of Analysis in Medical Care Experiments." *Medical Care*, 1984, *22* (12), 1101–1114.

Wholey, J. S. *Evaluation: Promise and Performance*. Washington, D.C.: Urban Institute, 1979.

Wholey, J. S. "Evaluability Assessment: Developing Program Theory." In L. Bickman (ed.), *Using Program Theory in Evaluation*. New Directions for Program Evaluation, no. 33. San Francisco: Jossey-Bass, 1987.

Kendon J. Conrad is an associate director of the Department of Veterans Affairs Health Services Research and Development Field Program, which serves four hospitals in the Chicago area; a research assistant professor at the Center for Health Services and Policy Research of Northwestern University in Evanston, Illinois; and an adjunct assistant professor in the School of Public Health at the University of Illinois, Chicago.

Janet R. Buelow is a research associate at the Brookdale Center on Aging, Hunter College/CUNY, New York.

A pattern-matching approach provides a useful framework for developing and testing program theory.

A Pattern-Matching Approach to Link Program Theory and Evaluation Data

Jules M. Marquart

Progress toward theory-based evaluation has been limited in part because few well-developed and practical methods are available for developing program theory and causal models in evaluation contexts. This is especially true for methods that involve having program stakeholders articulate their assumptions and explanations of the program. Yet, these implicit theories (McClintock, 1987) are essential for understanding the program and its objectives within an organizational and local context (Riggin, this volume). A further issue is how to test the theory in the actual program evaluation (Mark, this volume; Conrad and Buelow, this volume).

This chapter addresses these issues by describing how concept-mapping methods can be used for theory development, and how a pattern-matching approach (Marquart, 1988a, 1988b, 1989; Trochim 1985, 1989b) can be used to assess the congruence between the theory developed and the data from the evaluation. Pattern matching is used here to mean the correspondence between a theoretical or conceptual expectation pattern and an observed or measured pattern in the data. This approach builds on Campbell's (1966) notion that pattern matching between theory and data is a way of achieving scientific understanding. The value of a pattern match is that the validity of the conclusions drawn from the data is strength-

The author is grateful to Leonard Bickman, Valerie Caracelli, Charles McClintock, Leslie Riggin, and William Trochim for their helpful comments on an earlier draft of this chapter.

ened if the pattern of results predicted by the theory is found in the data; more complex patterns, if corroborated, provide more evidence for internal validity. And how do we get more complex patterns? By delineating the constructs more fully, that is, by preoperational explication of causes and effects, or better conceptualization. Greater effort on construct validity through conceptualization can lead to more precise, refined patterns of outcomes and thus improve internal validity (Trochim, 1985).

The pattern-matching approach is based on the interplay between the theoretical realm, which includes theories, ideas, and hunches about the program, and the observational realm, which is the pattern of data derived from the measures used to assess the program. As applied to program evaluation, the expected outcomes are contingent on (1) the nature of the program, (2) who the participants are, and (3) what is measured. Thus, for each major component of the evaluation—program, participants, measures, and outcomes—there are theoretical or conceptual patterns and observed patterns from the data, and the degree of correspondence between these patterns is called the pattern match. (See Conrad and Buelow, this volume, for another type of pattern matching.)

This chapter illustrates how a pattern-matching approach was applied to an evaluation of an employer-sponsored child care program. The study focused on obtaining (1) the *measurement* pattern match to provide evidence for construct validity of the evaluation instrument and (2) the *outcome* pattern match to assess the validity of the hypothesized causal relationship between the program and its outcomes. The rationale and procedures for the measurement and outcome pattern matches are explained, and issues involved in using this approach are discussed.

Background

Evaluation Context. The program being evaluated was an employer-sponsored child care program provided by a large medical complex in the Midwest. The focus of the evaluation was on employees' attitudes and behaviors that affected their performance and value to the organization, and not on the effects of the child care programs upon the child or the parent-child relationship.

Need for a "Theory" of the Program. Beyond the scope of the evaluation, I was interested in developing a program model that would define the linkages between employer-sponsored child care as a program, its processes, and its outcomes. Previous evaluations of child care programs found weak and inconsistent program effects (for example, Dawson, Mikel, Lorenz, and King, 1984; Krug, Palmour, and Ballassai, 1972; Milkovich and Gomez, 1976; Miller, 1984; Youngblood and Chambers-Cook, 1984). Their results implied that unrealistic assumptions were being made about the causal relationship between the program and its hypothesized outcomes and that insufficient attention had been paid to relationships among probable effects. I reasoned that, in an attempt to begin developing a theory of this program, it might be useful to tap the "implicit theories" of administrators in organizations that provide child care programs. I wanted the "theory" not only to reflect the specific program being evaluated but also to be generalizable across employer-sponsored child care programs.

To that end, managers in hospitals that provided child care programs were considered an appropriate stakeholder group from whom to obtain implicit or working theories of the program. Administrators were chosen because they have a perspective on the entire organization and are usually the decision makers responsible for authorizing such programs (McClintock, this volume).

Pattern-Matching Framework

The conceptual framework for developing the theoretical and observed patterns and for assessing the congruence or match between them is presented in Figure 1. The theoretical patterns are developed from the perspectives of the health administrators in hospitals that sponsor child care programs; the observed patterns are obtained from the data in the evaluation of the employer-sponsored child care program. The specific methods for assessing the measurement and outcome pattern matches are shown on the left-hand and right-hand sides of the figure, respectively.

Methods for Theory Development

Sample. Nine health administrators attending an annual professional development conference at Cornell University volunteered to participate in the study. They all were employed in hospitals that provided a child care program and considered themselves familiar with issues related to such programs.

Procedures. To obtain the health administrators' implicit theories of employer-sponsored child care programs, two procedures were used: (1) concept mapping to obtain their perceptions of the relationship between the program and pertinent concepts and (2) causal ratings to obtain their perceptions of the causal relationship between the program and its intended outcomes. In addition, a causal mapping exercise and an activity to have the administrators identify other organizational programs that were possible "causes" for the outcomes were conducted, but that part of the study is beyond the scope of this chapter (see Marquart, 1988b).

In concept mapping (Trochim, 1989a), concepts are sorted by a group to produce maps that graphically portray the group's perceptions of the relationships among the concepts or variables. The resulting maps are used as tools for eliciting the group's interpretation and explanations of the relationships among the concepts.

The concept-mapping component provides the foundation for address-

Figure 1. Conceptual Framework for Theoretical and Observed Patterns

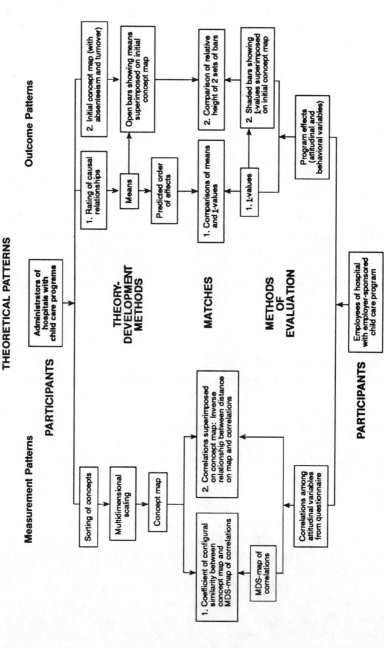

ing the construct validity of the variables measured, while the causal rating yield an implied theory for assessing the internal validity of the causal effects of the program.

Data Collection. Two sessions with the health administrators were held, the first to conduct the sorting and rating activities, and the second to obtain their interpretations and explanations of the concept maps and causal ratings.

The selection of the concepts used in the sorting and rating activities was based on related variables mentioned most often in the literature and on the variables being measured in the evaluation. This meant that the "theory" being tested was a mixture of research-based concepts and experientially based interpretation of those concepts (see Valentine, 1989). The following concepts were used: (1) *attitudinal:* recruitment, job satisfaction, organizational commitment, satisfaction with child care arrangement, stress regarding child care, and stress in balancing work and family; (2) *behavioral:* absenteeism and turnover; and (3) *organizational or structural:* organization's personnel policies, supervisor's personnel practices, and employer-sponsored child care.

In the sorting procedure, each administrator was given a set of cards with the concept names and asked to sort them into piles according to their similarity, that is, according to which ones in his or her opinion belonged together.

In the rating activity, the administrators were given a list of the variables in the study and were asked to consider if they regarded employer-sponsored child care programs as having a causal effect on any of the variables. For each variable that they considered a possible program effect, the participants used values from 1 (no or weak relationship) to 100 (strong) to rate the strength of the causal relationship between the child care program and the outcomes.

Data Analysis. Multidimensional scaling (MDS) analyses were conducted on the sorted data to produce the concept map; a two-dimensional map was chosen for its ease of use and interpretability (Kruskal and Wish, 1978). The map shows the administrators' perceptions of the relationships among the concepts and represents the *theoretical measurement pattern.*

From the causal ratings, means and standard deviations were calculated for the ratings of each concept as an effect of employer-sponsored child care. The mean values represent the order of effects predicted by the administrators and can be considered the *theoretical outcome pattern.*

Methods of the Program Evaluation

A quasi-experimental design was used to compare the users and nonusers of the employer-sponsored child care program on their work-related attitudes (for example, job satisfaction and organizational commitment) and the behaviors of absenteeism and turnover. Data on the attitudinal variables were collected by a questionnaire mailed to the program users and nonus-ers one-and-one-half years after the program began. Data on absenteeism and turnover were collected from personnel records. Turnover was mea-sured for the first year of the program; absenteeism data were compared for one year prior to the program and the first two years of the program.

The data from the child care program evaluation were treated in two ways. First, correlations were obtained between the variables measured on the questionnaire. Then, MDS analysis was conducted on the correlations, just as it was for the sorting data, to produce a concept map of the correla-tions, which is referred to as the MDS map of correlations in Figure 1. Such a map portrays graphically the relationships among the variables from the correlations and represents the *observed measurement pattern*.

T-tests (and F-tests for absenteeism) comparing program users and nonusers were conducted on the outcome variables. The resulting t-values are used as the measure of the strength of the effect of the program on each variable in the evaluation and represent the *observed outcome pattern*.

Measurement Pattern Matching

Theoretical Measurement Pattern
The concept map in Figure 2 shows the administrators' perceptions of the relationships among the concepts. (It uses only the variables measured on the questionnaire—excluding absenteeism and turnover, and employer-sponsored child care as the independent variable—to facilitate comparison with the MDS map of the correlations between the variables from the questionnaire, presented in Figure 3.) Since location on the map is a function of perceived similarity, the concepts that were most frequently sorted together are closest to each other, and those that were seldom or never sorted together are farthest apart or on opposite sides of the map. Three groups of concepts stand out on the map: one group with concepts referring to work attitudes (job satisfaction and organizational commit-ment), a second with the concepts pertaining to child care issues (the two stress concepts and child care satisfaction), and a third linking recruitment with personnel policies and practices.

Observed Measurement Pattern
The map in Figure 3 is the MDS map of the correlations from the question-naire used to measure the employees' attitudes in the evaluation. This map shows four groups of variables: one group pertaining to stress; a second with work attitudes (job satisfaction and organizational commitment); a third with the personnel variables; and a fourth with recruitment and child care satisfaction. For the first three groups, the pairs of variables that were most highly correlated with each other formed their own distinct clusters. Child care satisfaction, which was most strongly correlated with the two

Figure 2. Concept Map from Sorting of Concepts by Administrators

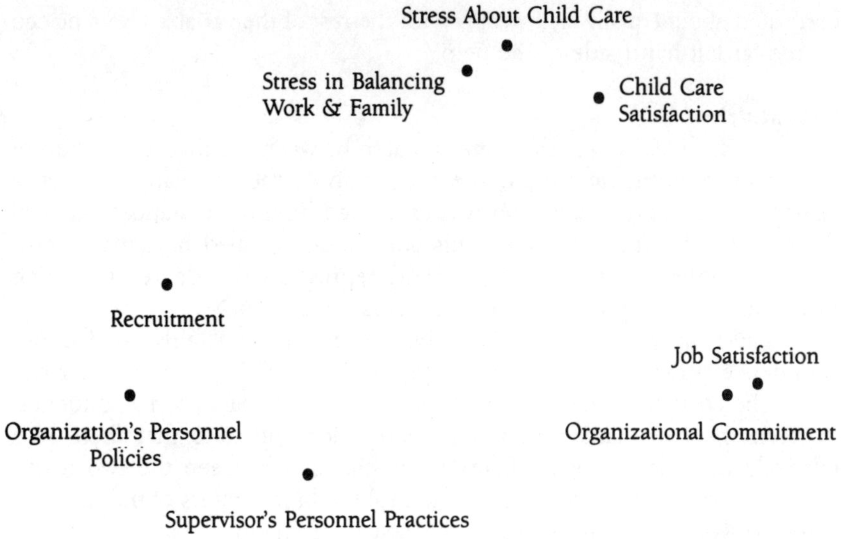

Stress About Child Care

Stress in Balancing
Work & Family

Child Care
Satisfaction

Recruitment

Job Satisfaction

Organization's Personnel
Policies

Organizational Commitment

Supervisor's Personnel Practices

Figure 3. Multidimensional Scaling Map of Correlations from Evaluation Questionnaire

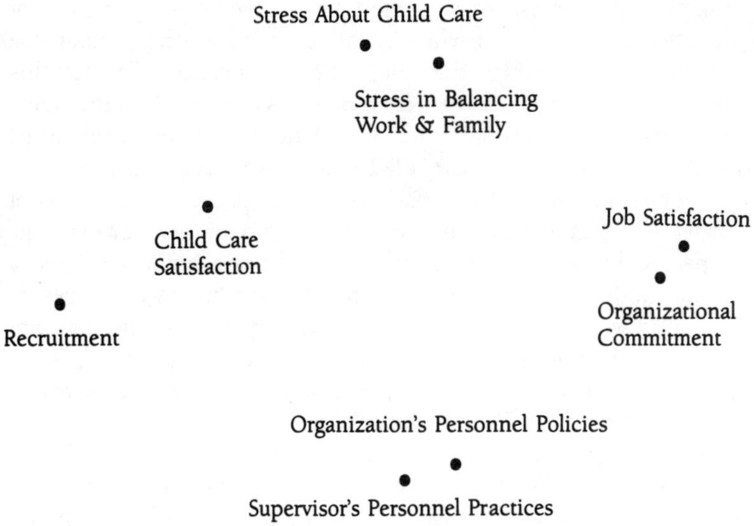

Stress About Child Care

Stress in Balancing
Work & Family

Child Care
Satisfaction

Job Satisfaction

Organizational
Commitment

Recruitment

Organization's Personnel Policies

Supervisor's Personnel Practices

stress variables and the organization's personnel policies, was placed at roughly an equal distance from those concepts. Recruitment, which was correlated about equally and weakly with the rest of the variables, was placed on the far left-hand side of the map.

First Match

Procedures. To assess the pattern match between the theoretical map of the health administrators and the MDS map of the correlational data, a Pearson's correlation coefficient was calculated from the distances between the concepts on the two maps. This correlation is called here the "coefficient of configurational similarity" and represents the degree to which distances between points on the two maps are similar.

Results. By visual comparison, there seems to be a fairly good correspondence between the theoretical map and the MDS map of the correlations. The coefficient of configurational similarity, or spatial correspondence, between the two maps is .76. This correlation indicates that there is a relatively high degree of configurational similarity between the two maps, that is, between the perceptions of the health administrators of the relationships between the concepts and the actual correlational pattern between those same variables from the questionnaire.

Second Match

Procedures. Using the principles of convergence and discrimination from the multitrait-multimethod approach to construct validation (Campbell and Fiske, 1959; for an application to pattern matching, see Davis, 1989), one might expect that the variables located closer together on the concept map would be more highly correlated, and conversely, the greater the distance between the variables the lower their correlation. To test this assumption, the correlations between each pair of variables from the questionnaire were plotted on the theoretical map. The number of correlational relationships that confirmed the expected pattern were then counted.

Results. Figure 4 shows the correlations superimposed on the concept map. In order to visually differentiate the strength of the correlations, different types of lines are used: a solid line for the highest values, a broken line for moderate values, and a dotted line for the lowest values.

The variables *within* each of the three distinct groups on the map are more highly correlated with each other than with variables in other groups. Of the twenty-eight pairs of correlations, there is only one exception (between job satisfaction and stress in balancing work and family) to this confirming pattern of relationships. Another way of considering these patterns of relationships is that the variables that are more highly correlated with each other are located closer to each other on the map, while those with lower correlations are farther apart on the map. Thus, an inverse relationship between distance on the map and the strength of the correlations can be observed in this figure.

**Figure 4. Correlations from Evaluation Questionnaire
Superimposed on Concept Map**

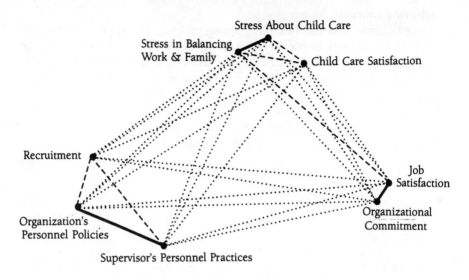

Note: Solid line = high correlation (.41-.60); broken line = moderate correlation (.21-.40); dotted line = low correlation (.01-.20).

Summary

Overall, a fairly high degree of correspondence was found between the administrators' perceptions of the relationships between the concepts related to employer-sponsored child care and the correlations among the variables on the questionnaire. Because the pattern of relationships among the variables on the measurement instrument reflects the theoretical patterns among the concepts, this match provides evidence for the construct validity of the evaluation questionnaire.

Outcome Pattern Matching

The outcome pattern match assesses the correspondence between the order of effects predicted by the health administrators and the actual order of effects found in the program evaluation.

Theoretical Outcome Pattern

As shown in Figure 5, the health administrators predicted that satisfaction with child care and job satisfaction would be most affected and that absenteeism and turnover would be least affected by employer-sponsored child care; the remaining variables were rated as being moderately affected by child care programs. Two variables, the organization's personnel policies and supervisor's personnel practices, were not perceived to be program effects and are not included in subsequent comparisons.

Observed Outcome Pattern

The evaluation data indicated that strong program effects (with statistically significant differences between the program users and nonusers) were on recruitment, stress about child care, and satisfaction with child care arrangement (Figure 5). Weak program effects (with nonsignificant group differences) were found on the remaining variables.

**Figure 5. Outcome Pattern Match Between
Predicted and Actual Order of Effects**

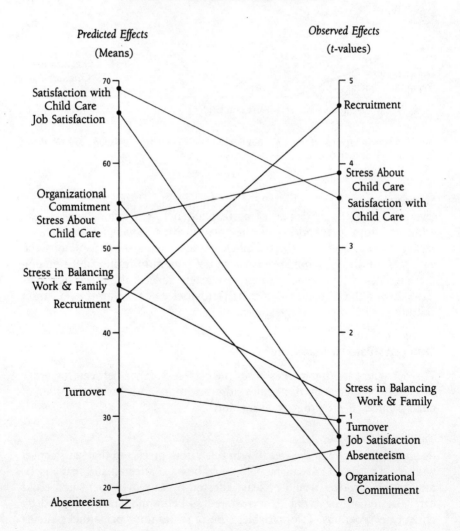

First Match

Procedures. A graphic representation of the two patterns was constructed by lining up the predicted and observed order of effects in columns, side by side, and drawing lines between the two. A Spearman correlation coefficient was calculated between the predicted means and observed t-values.

Results. As seen in Figure 5, there was fairly good correspondence between the predicted and observed patterns for four variables: satisfaction with child care and stress about child care as strong effects, and absenteeism and turnover as weak effects. It seems reasonable that the administrators would perceive the two child care variables to be most affected by the program, and, in fact, strong effects on those two variables were found in the evaluation. On the other hand, there was poor correspondence between the predicted and obtained patterns for job satisfaction and organizational commitment, which were perceived to be strong effects but were found to be weak effects, and for recruitment, value of which as an effect was underestimated.

The many crossover lines reveal the discrepancy between the mean ratings and the t-values. This lack of parallelism indicates a relatively poor match between the predicted and obtained outcome patterns. The correlation between the means and the t-values was .23, also showing the weak correspondence between them.

Second Match

Procedures. A second way of assessing the outcome pattern match was to superimpose a visual representation of the means and t-values on a concept map that includes absenteeism and turnover, since they are needed for the outcome patterns, and to determine how well the two patterns correspond. The initial concept map with all eleven variables that were sorted is presented in Figure 6. Recall that the organization's personnel policies and supervisor's personnel practices (and employer-sponsored child care) are not utilized because they were not rated as program effects. Open boxes representing the means and shaded boxes representing the t-values for each variable were appropriately scaled and placed next to each other by the same concept on the map. Stacked, open and shaded boxes that correspond relatively well in height indicate a successful match between the predicted and observed outcome patterns.

Second Match. In Figure 6, the predicted and observed patterns were most similar for stress related for child care, absenteeism, and satisfaction with child care arrangement. The predicted outcomes were much higher than the observed values for three variables; job satisfaction, organizational commitment, and stress in balancing work and family. For only one variable—recruitment—was the observed pattern greater than the predicted one; in the evaluation, recruitment was found to be the strongest effect of the program.

Figure 6. Means and *t*-Values of Outcome Pattern Match Superimposed on Concept Map

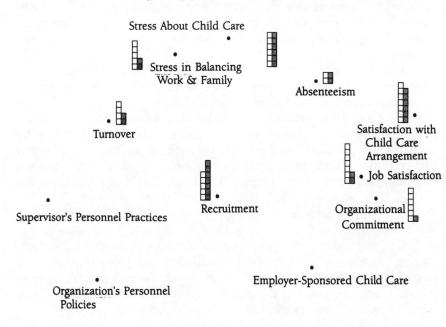

Stress About Child Care

Stress in Balancing Work & Family

Absenteeism

Turnover

Satisfaction with Child Care Arrangement

Job Satisfaction

Supervisor's Personnel Practices

Recruitment

Organizational Commitment

Organization's Personnel Policies

Employer-Sponsored Child Care

Note: Open boxes = means, and shaded boxes = *t*-values, using the following key for ranges:

Means	*t*-values
61–70	4.2–4.8
51–60	3.5–4.1
41–50	2.8–3.4
31–40	2.1–2.7
21–30	1.4–2.0
11–20	.7–1.3
0–10	0–0.6

Summary

There was limited correspondence found between the administrators' predicted order of effects and the actual order of effects in the program evaluation. The implied theory of the causal effects of the program was not supported by the empirical data, at least in the ways measured here.

Conclusion

A fairly high degree of correspondence was found between the health administrators' perceptions of the relationships between the concepts related to employer-sponsored child care (theoretical measurement pattern) and the correlations from the child care program evaluation (observed measurement pattern). This finding was supported both by the high coefficient of conceptual similarity, $r = .76$ (Figures 2 and 3) and by the inverse relationship found for the distances between the points on the concept map and the correlations (Figure 4). This successful measurement pattern match provides evidence for the construct validity of the survey questionnaire. The pattern of correlations among the variables as measured in the evaluation corresponded well to the pattern of relationships perceived by a diverse group of health administrators knowledgeable about such programs, who were working with research-based concepts.

However, in both ways tested (Figures 5 and 6), a high correspondence was not found between the outcomes predicted by the health administrators to be most affected by employer-sponsored child care and the actual order of effects found in the child care programs evaluation. This finding does not provide evidence for the validity of the causal hypothesis as held by the administrators. When a pattern match is not found, as in this case, several explanations are possible: (1) The health administrators may be "wrong" or may be too diverse in their opinions. (2) The health administrators are correct, but the conceptualization method or methods used to assess the match do not show it. Or (3) the health administrators are correct, but the evaluation data are too variable.

Initially, the purpose of obtaining the implicit theories of the administrators was to provide a more generalizable theory about employer-sponsored child care. However, the health administrators were a heterogeneous group whose ratings reflect their own hospital contexts to a large degree. There were considerable differences in the ratings for some of the variables, indicating that widely diverse opinions were held. Perhaps the predictions of the administrators would have proved more accurate in their own settings, as one might expect that different patterns of effects of employer-sponsored child care programs occur across organizations. This discrepancy illustrates the distinction that Conrad and Buelow (this volume) make between the theory of a program and how that program is actually operationalized as a project in a particular setting. It further points out that theorizing about a program takes place on different levels (social scientist, evaluator, program administrator, program recipient, and so on), and that taking into consideration what the different levels of program theory may contribute is important (Riggin, this volume). In this case, better predictions might have resulted from obtaining the implicit theories of stakeholders involved in the local program being evaluated.

Of course, it could also be that a match was not obtained because of the type of measurement here. The significance of effects, represented by the t-values, may not be the best criterion for assessing a match with predicted effects. For example, significant effects could have been found on all the variables in the evaluation, yet if the administrators had predicted a different pattern of effects, no match would have been shown. On another level, these differences illustrate the way in which empirical data can contradict assumptions about how human service programs work and what effects can reasonably be expected (Schwarz, 1980), thus pointing out the importance of obtaining the implicit theories of program stakeholders in the conceptualization and implementation of a program evaluation (McClintock, 1986). Better ways are needed both to develop conceptual structures of a complex program and to assess the correspondence between those theoretical patterns and patterns in the data (see Mark, this volume; Smith, this volume).

The difference in success between the measurement and outcome pattern matches also suggests that it is easier to define relationships among constructs in the conceptual domain than it is to specify causal relationships between them. Causality remains as difficult a notion to deal with in the evaluation of employer-sponsored child care as it is with other complex service delivery systems.

Despite the mixed success in obtaining measurement and outcome pattern matches, these methods deserve consideration as initial attempts to develop program theory from the perspective of program stakeholders and to incorporate program theory into evaluation design. The pattern-matching approach in this study offers methods for developing and testing theory in program evaluation and, furthermore, provides a useful framework for assessing both construct and internal validity in applied evaluation contexts.

References

Campbell, D. T. "Pattern Matching as an Essential in Distal Knowing." In K. R. Hammond (ed.), *The Psychology of Egon Brunswick*. New York: Holt, Rinehart & Winston, 1966.

Campbell, D. T., and Fiske, D. W. "Convergent and Discriminant Validation by the Multitrait-Multimethod Matrix." *Psychological Bulletin*, 1959, 56 (2), 81–105.

Davis, J. E. "Construct Validity in Measurement: A Pattern Matching Approach." *Evaluation and Program Planning*, 1989, 12 (1), 31–36.

Dawson, A. G., Mikel, C. S., Lorenz, C. S., and King, J. *An Experimental Study of the Effects of Employer-Sponsored Child Care Services on Selected Employee Behaviors.* Washington, D.C.: Department of Health and Human Services, Office of Human Development Services, 1984.

Krug, D. N., Palmour, V. E., and Ballassai, M. C. *Evaluation of the Office of Economic Opportunity Child Development Center.* Rockville, Md.: Westat, 1972.

Kruskal, J. B., and Wish, M. *Multidimensional Scaling.* Newbury Park, Calif.: Sage, 1978.

McClintock, C. "Toward a Theory of Formative Evaluation." In M. W. Lipsey and D. S. Cordray (eds.), *Evaluation Studies Review Annual.* Vol. 11. Newbury Park, Calif.: Sage, 1986.

McClintock, C. "Conceptual and Action Heuristics: Tools for the Evaluator." In L. Bickman (ed.), *Using Program Theory in Evaluation.* New Directions for Program Evaluation, no. 33. San Francisco: Jossey-Bass, 1987.

Marquart, J. M. "Measurement and Outcome Pattern Matches: Examples from an Employer-Sponsored Child Care Program Evaluation." Paper presented at the annual meeting of the American Evaluation Association, New Orleans, October 29, 1988a.

Marquart, J. M. "A Pattern Matching Approach to Link Program Theory and Evaluation Data: The Case of Employer-Sponsored Child Care." Unpublished doctoral dissertation, Cornell University, 1988b.

Marquart, J. M. "A Pattern Matching Approach to Assess the Construct Validity of an Evaluation Instrument." *Evaluation and Program Planning*, 1989, *12* (1), 37–43.

Milkovich, G. T., and Gomez, L. R. "Day Care and Selected Work Behaviors." *Academy of Management Journal*, 1976, *19* (1), 111–115.

Miller, T. I. "The Effects of Employer-Sponsored Child Care on Employee Absenteeism, Turnover, Productivity, Recruitment or Job Satisfaction: What Is Claimed and What Is Known." *Personnel Psychology*, 1984, *37*, 277–289.

Schwarz, P. A. "Program Devaluation: Can the Experiment Reform?" In E. Loveland (ed.), *Measuring the Hard to Measure*. New Directions for Program Evaluation, no. 6. San Francisco: Jossey-Bass, 1980.

Trochim, W.M.K. "Pattern Matching, Validity, and Conceptualization in Program Evaluation." *Evaluation Review*, 1985, *9*, 575–604.

Trochim, W.M.K. "An Introduction to Concept Mapping for Planning and Evaluation." *Evaluation and Program Planning*, 1989a, *12* (1), 1–16.

Trochim, W.M.K. "Pattern Matching and Program Theory." *Evaluation and Program Planning*, 1989b, *12* (4), 355–366.

Valentine, K. "Contributions to the Theory of Care." *Evaluation and Program Planning*, 1989, *12* (1), 17–25.

Youngblood, S. A., and Chambers-Cook, K. "Child Care Assistance Can Improve Employee Attitudes and Behavior." *Personnel Administrator*, Feb. 1984, pp. 45–46, 93–95.

Jules M. Marquart is a research associate at the Foundation for Human Service Studies in Ithaca, New York. Her research and consulting are in the areas of program evaluation, child care, and work and family linkages.

Social science theory can strengthen the conceptualization and interpretation of program theory-based evaluation.

Linking Program Theory and Social Science Theory

Leslie J. C. Riggin

Chen (this volume) has proposed an integrative approach to program theory-based evaluation. The integrative approach combines theories of program stakeholders and social science theory to construct strong program theories. This chapter discusses and illustrates some specific benefits of linking local program theory, as held by program stakeholders, to social science theory. The first section of the chapter describes the articulation and evaluation of the theory underlying an employment and training program for welfare recipients. Then, looking at the evaluation in retrospect, the second section considers how social science theory could have affected the conceptualization of the evaluation and the interpretation of the findings. The chapter concludes with a discussion of issues in the linkage of program theory and social science theory.

Evaluation Context

The evaluation described here examined the implementation of a state-administered employment assistance program for recipients of Aid to Families with Dependent Children (AFDC) and/or food stamps. Some welfare recipients, those living in remote areas or caring for children under age three, for example, are exempt from participation in the program. Those

The author thanks Leonard Bickman, Valerie Caracelli, and Jules Marquart for providing helpful comments on an earlier draft of this chapter. The evaluation described in the chapter was not conducted at GAO, and the statements and opinions expressed do not represent official GAO policy.

who are not exempt are required to participate in organized activities designed to improve their employability and to support their search for employment. The most common activities are Individual Job Search, in which clients are assisted in looking for a job, and Education, in which clients attend classes in adult basic education, literacy, or job skills. If a client does not comply with the participation requirement, he or she can be sanctioned through a termination of or reduction in his or her food stamp or AFDC grant.

In 1987, the first year of the program's operation, program managers initiated an evaluation of the implementation of the employment assistance program. The purpose of the evaluation was to inform decisions about program improvements and to consider the program as a plausible explanation of outcomes in a planned summative evaluation. The implementation of the participation requirement was of special interest because the previous employment assistance program had been criticized for "creaming," serving those clients who were most likely to succeed, rather than those most in need of services.

The evaluator framed the evaluation as a test of implementation theory, examining what procedures had been applied and the processes through which they worked (Finney and Moos, 1989; Scheirer, 1987). First, models of how the program was intended to operate were developed. These models were then compared to data on the program in operation. The congruencies and discrepancies between the program as intended and the program in operation provided the basis for conclusions and recommendations.

Conceptualizing the Evaluation. Program theory was selected as the conceptual basis of the evaluation for two reasons. First, the evaluator expected that program theory would enhance the relevance, and hence the utilization, of the evaluation (Bickman, 1987; Leviton and Hughes, 1981; McClintock, 1987). Second, review of evaluations of similar programs and literature on theories of participation in adult education and training programs did not provide an appropriate theoretical baseline for the evaluation. The evaluations tended to focus on impacts, while the theories of client participation were not readily applicable to situations in which participation is mandatory. In combination with the evaluator's concern for the relevance of the evaluation, the lack of germane social science theory led to the choice of program theory for the theoretical baseline of the evaluation.

In order to articulate the theory underlying the program, documents from the employment assistance program were reviewed and used to derive three models: (1) intended client flow through the program, (2) intended relationships among program components and objectives, and (3) theoretical causal linkages between mandatory participation and program outcomes. These models were distributed to program managers, who were asked to provide feedback. The models were then refined, based on the responses of the managers.

Although only the third model delineated causal relationships, all three program models described the theory underlying the employment assistance program. The models of client flow through the program and of the relationships between program components are the kinds of models used in evaluability assessment to clarify intended administrative procedures and their relationship to program objectives (Wholey, 1987). These models reflect administrators' hypotheses about how program resources and procedures fit together to bring about program objectives (McClintock, this volume). In contrast, the model of the linkages between mandatory participation and program outcomes focused on the underlying process through which program outcomes were expected to be achieved.

This third model, showing the theoretical role of mandatory participation in the program provides an illustration of the use of program theory as the conceptual foundation of the evaluation. The model is displayed in Figure 1.

The two assumptions underlying the participation requirement are (1) because of the threat of sanctions, clients who need the AFDC or food stamp benefits will participate and (2) those clients who do not participate have alternatives to public assistance and will be "weeded out" by sanctions. If these assumptions are true, mandatory participation could enable the employment assistance program to reach its primary objective of saving state and federal dollars by reducing the caseload. Caseload can be reduced either through sanctions or through client employment.

The three program theory models guided data collection on the program in operation. The evaluator not only focused on program components and processes that were specified in the models but also looked for program variables and relationships that were not included. For example, the model of mandatory participation focused data collection efforts on unin-

Figure 1. Local Theory Underlying the Employment Assistance Program

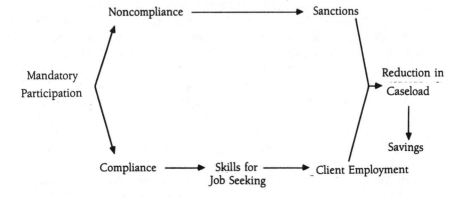

tended side-effects of mandatory participation, as well as on the implementation of the participation requirement and the linkage between mandatory participation and compliance.

A combination of quantitative and qualitative methods was used for complementarity purposes (Greene, Caracelli, and Graham, 1989) and provided information on program operations and client characteristics. Qualitative data were collected from interviews of employment counselors and clients and from observations of program activities. That data were organized into categories relating to the variables and relationships identified in the program theory models. In addition, new variables and relationships emerged from the data. For example, environmental variables, such as the availability of public transportation and the local labor market, other program variables, such as the way the eligibility workers presented the program to clients, and variables in clients' personal situations were identified and linked to the decision to comply or not comply with the program's participation requirement. The inductive content analysis of the qualitative data resulted in a narrative description of the program in operation. The quantitative data, collected through review of client records, were used to enhance and clarify the results of the qualitative analysis by describing the client population and the extent of participation and nonparticipation in the program.

Interpreting the Data on the Program in Operation. Using a pattern-matching approach (Marquart, this volume; Trochim, 1985, 1989), the description of the program's implementation was compared to the models of the program as intended. The program theory models were then revised to depict the variables and relationships that were found empirically. For example, in light of the data on the program in operation, the model portrayed in Figure 1 was elaborated. Figure 2 represents the revised model of the role of mandatory participation in the program.

As can be seen in this figure, the data on the program in operation confirmed the role of mandatory participation in program processes. However, the data also specified additional independent and mediating variables in the program. The independent variables that emerged were classified as contextual, program, or client factors. Contextual factors include the extent of employment and educational opportunities and the availability of public transportation in the area. Reimbursements for transportation and child care and the behavior of program staff toward the clients were among the program variables that moderated the role of mandatory participation. Client variables include literacy, health, work experience, and personal motivation. Depending on the intensity and direction of these other influences, the participation requirement could be either reinforced or undermined.

The data on the program in operation revealed an initial client reaction to the participation requirement and other antecedent conditions.

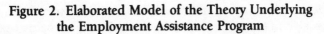

Figure 2. Elaborated Model of the Theory Underlying
the Employment Assistance Program

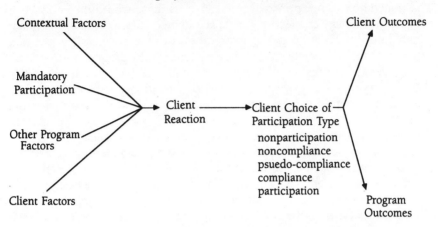

While many clients responded with acceptance of the program's requirements, other client responses were fear of change, motivation in response to the perception of opportunities, and resentment over the mandatory nature of the program. These initial reactions help explain the subsequent participation behaviors.

The original model depicted only two possible client behaviors: compliance or noncompliance. In contrast, the elaborated model incorporates a range of participation types: nonparticipation, noncompliance, pseudo-compliance, compliance, and true participation. Nonparticipation refers to the situation in which a client does not attend even the initial informational meeting conducted by the program. Noncompliance differs from nonparticipation in that clients have some interaction with the program (and therefore may be expected to understand both the services of the program and the sanctions for nonparticipation) before they decide not to participate. While this distinction emerged in the data, the program considers these two behaviors equally and noncompliance.

Similarly, pseudo-compliance, compliance, and true participation were treated as compliance by the program (except in the rare cases where pseudo-compliance was discovered by program staff, in which instance it was treated as noncompliance). Pseudo-compliance refers to the situation in which a client feigns compliance in order to retain his or her benefits. Compliance occurs when a client does what is required but does not seek the services of the program beyond what is required. At the extreme is true participation in which the client interacts with the program beyond its requirements, by seeking advice from the employment counselor, for example.

Further, the data revealed both program and client outcomes that were not included in the original program theory. For example, in some areas, the participation requirement led to a larger caseload than the program was able to serve. In such situations, the program neither sanctioned all noncompliers nor provided services to all those who did comply. As a result, the inability to effectively serve all required clients, with a consequent inability to change the public assistance caseload, are possible program outcomes that were not included in the model of the program as intended.

Client outcomes, besides employment or reduced benefits, were also identified. For example, some clients continued dependence on public assistance, without being sanctioned or employed. Many clients met the participation requirements of the program without finding employment, while others did not comply and were not sanctioned because of paperwork delays or errors. Another client outcome not included in the original program model is the improvement of a client's situation in ways not directly related to employment. For example, employment counselors occasionally helped ill clients obtain treatment. More commonly, clients received education or training services that they might not otherwise have pursued. Especially in the rural areas, this additional training did not necessarily lead to employment but was nonetheless deemed an important client outcome by both clients and service providers.

Overall, data on the program in operation did not so much diverge from the original program model as they did clarify and elaborate on it. The original model is embedded in the revised model. But the revised model suggests that, in the implementation of the employment assistance program, the linkages between mandatory participation and the desired program outcomes are neither as strong nor as clear as intended.

The results of the evaluation were presented to the program managers and used as a basis for discussing recommendations for bringing the program in theory and the program in operation into congruence. The recommendations included changes to program theory as well as to program operations. For example, a recommended change to the theory was the inclusion of the contextual variables that affect program processes and outcomes. Within certain contexts, such as rural areas with few support services or employment opportunities, the program managers could modify the desired outcomes to account for environmental constraints. On the other hand, to bring program operations in line with the theory, the linkage between noncompliance and sanctioning needed to be strengthened. The options of limiting participation by specifying priority groups, hiring additional employment counselors, or devising more effective tools for closely monitoring client activities so noncompliance could be easily identified by the counselors were considered. In this case, program managers found that it was both possible and desirable to increase the number of employment counselors.

In short, the articulation of local program theory in the form of models was a fruitful conceptualization technique, directing the evaluator to specific, relevant areas of inquiry. The subsequent matching of patterns in the data on the program in operation with models of the program as intended facilitated the interpretation of the findings. Moreover, the use of local program theory as a theoretical baseline encouraged the utilization of the evaluation by program managers (Riggin, 1990).

The next section examines how this evaluation might have been conducted differently if social science theory had informed the development and evaluation of the program theory models. Although the conceptualization phase of the evaluation did not discover any specifically germane social science theories, Etzioni's (1975) theory of compliance subsequently appeared applicable to certain aspects of the employment assistance program. The following discussion uses this theory to illustrate how social science theory and program theory can be linked in the practice of evaluation.

The Role of Social Science Theory in Conceptualization

Social science theory can inform program theory at both the conceptualization and interpretation phases of an evaluation. In conceptualization, a theoretical foundation in local program theory can enhance the relevance of the evaluation to program stakeholders. However, social science theory can further specify the conceptual domain by identifying additional variables and their interrelationships. Detailed conceptual patterns are the first step in providing evidence for construct validity (Campbell and Fiske, 1959; Trochim 1985, 1989). The elaboration of program theory with social science theory provides a richer pattern of relationships between variables than is possible with a less-articulated theoretical pattern. If the pattern of theoretical relationships is mirrored in the data, the argument for the construct validity of the program is stronger than if the original theoretical pattern is less detailed. As an illustration of the potential role of social science theory in the conceptualization of an evaluation based on program theory, consider how Etzioni's (1975) theory of compliance might have changed the evaluation described above.

Etzioni (1975) developed a model of compliance to explain the relationship of individuals within organizations. He defines compliance as "a relationship consisting of the power employed by superiors to control subordinates and the orientation of the subordinates to this power" (Etzioni, 1975, p. xii). Of note in this definition is the conceptualization of compliance as a relationship rather than as a behavior.

As a relationship, compliance consists of two dimensions: the type of power wielded by the superior and the orientation of the subordinate. Etzioni describes three types of power: coercive, remunerative, and normative. Coercive power consists of control through physical sanctions or through the satisfaction of basic needs, such as the need for food. Remunerative power rests on control over material resources and rewards, such as salaries. Normative power consists of the power to allocate symbolic rewards and deprivations.

In the original model of the employment assistance program, power is represented by the participation requirement, undergirded by the ability to apply sanctions. This power could be labeled either coercive or remunerative, depending on the extent of the client's need. Normative power does not appear in the original model. However, normative power is a source of authority in the employment assistance program. Specifically, eligibility workers and employment counselors have control over the respect with which a client is treated in the context of the program. The data on the program in operation indicated that the behavior of both the eligibility workers and the employment counselors toward clients had an effect on client response to the program.

Prior knowledge of Etzioni's typology of power would have attuned the evaluator to the varieties of control being employed in the program, thus focusing the data collection and enriching her understanding of the program's operations. Moreover, if the typology of power had been used to elaborate the original model of the program as theoretically conceived, there would have been a better match between the program in theory and the data on the program in operation. This congruence would have strengthened claims of the construct validity of the program (Trochim, 1985, 1989). Finally, if Etzioni's theory had been included in the conceptualization of the evaluation, the evaluation could have tested the applicability of the global theory in a local context.

The Role of Social Science Theory in Interpretation

Social science theory can contribute to evaluation based on program theory not only in the conceptualization phase but also in the interpretation of evaluation findings. While similarities between the program in operation and the program in theory provide evidence for the construct validity of the program, similarities between evaluation findings and social science theory support claims of the external validity of the evaluation (Campbell, 1986; Yin, 1984). When social science theory supports or further explains evaluation findings, there is evidence for the robustness of the findings at different levels of generalization. The following example illustrates how interpretation of program data in the framework of a broader theory can clarify the findings. The potential for tests of local theory to contribute to the development of social science theory is also discussed.

As described above, the data on the implementation of the employment assistance program revealed an initial client reaction to the program that was not present in the original program model. This client reaction can be interpreted in the framework of Etzioni's theory as the subordinate's orientation to power. The orientation of the subordinate to the type of power is conceptualized by Etzioni as a continuum. The extreme negative orientation is alienation and the extreme positive orientation is moral commitment. In the middle of the continuum is calculative orientation, which takes both positive and negative forms. Unlike alienation or moral commitment, a calculative orientation is characterized by the low intensity of the subordinate's involvement in the compliance relationship. The orientation of the subordinate tends to parallel the type of power used to achieve organizational goals. In other words, coercive power will be met with alienation while normative power will be met with moral commitment.

In examining the relationship between the type of power and the orientation of the subordinate in the employment assistance program, a comparison of the initial client reactions to the continuum of orientations suggests that, in general, clients had a calculative orientation. That is, most clients appeared to comply with the participation requirement without strong feelings about either the program's sanctions or its services. In the framework of the larger theory, this orientation implies that the type of power being used was remunerative rather than coercive or normative. In other words, the participation requirement was neither so coercive that it alienated clients, nor so inspiring that clients adopted the goals of the program. Instead (with exceptions on both extremes), clients did what the program required in order to retain their benefits.

While the compliance theory sheds light on the relationship between type of power and client orientation, it is less useful in explaining why the program appeared ineffective in achieving its goals. In Etzioni's theory, an organization should be effective in achieving its goals when the type of power used is consistent with the goals of the program. In the employment assistance program, remunerative power is consistent with the largely economic goals of the program: hence, the program should achieve its objectives. However, the linkages between the requirement to participate and the desired program outcome of reduced caseload were weak. Since a mismatch between the type of power employed and the goals of the program was not in evidence, the theory does not explain why the program did not seem to be achieving its objectives. But, the data on the program in operation suggest two reasons. First, the power formally employed by the program, the sanctions for nonparticipation, were not implemented as intended. As stated before, because of the large caseloads, some noncompliers were not sanctioned. Second, contextual factors, particularly the lack of jobs, inhibited the employment of clients. The theory of compliance neither addresses situations in which the type of power is not implemented as intended nor includes environmental constraints on achieving organizational goals.

In summary, Etzioni's theory helps the interpretation of the relationship between the program and the initial client response by highlighting the congruence of the two. In this case, where evaluation findings match social science theory, the evidence for the external validity of the results is strengthened. Because of its congruence with Etzioni's well-established and tested theory, the compliance relationship found between mandatory participation and client acceptance of the requirement is likely to be generalizable to other situations.

But the theory was less helpful in explaining why linkages between program inputs and intended program outcomes were weak. In this kind of situation, evaluation results may inform social science theory by generating new theoretical propositions. The generalizability of these propositions can then be tested in other studies. For example, in the employment assistance program, environmental factors limited the effectiveness of the compliance relationship in achieving program goals. Future studies of Etzioni's theory could further explicate the role of environmental factors in the compliance relationship.

Linking Program Theory and Social Science Theory

The above illustrations demonstrate how linking program theory and social science theory in the context of an evaluation can not only enhance the practice of evaluation but also facilitate the use of evaluation results for the development and refinement of social science theory. Notwithstanding this positive assessment of the potential for the integrative approach, there are still many issues involved in linking program theory and social science theory. Two of the major issues are briefly considered here.

The appropriate role of social science theory in evaluations based on program theory is still being debated (Chen and Rossi, 1983, 1987; Finney and Moos, 1989; Trochim, 1985). Chen and Rossi (1983) have argued for the primacy of social science theory in theory-driven evaluation. In contrast, this chapter supports a foundation in program theory, supplemented by social science theory when feasible and appropriate. Program theory can improve utilization by enhancing the relevance of the evaluation to program stakeholders. It focuses the evaluator on the implementation of the program, thus avoiding the black box problems of old. Finally, program theory is always available, if one take the time to elicit it from program stakeholders. In calling for theory-driven evaluation, Chen and Rossi (1983) and Chen (1990) argue against the uncritical acceptance of local stakeholders' views as the conceptual basis of an evaluation. However, a conceptual foundation in local program theory does not imply the uncritical acceptance of that theory. Instead, the critical use of program theory is achieved by its comparison to empirical evidence. The integrative approach, in which stakeholders' theories of the program and social science theories are articulated and used to discuss the appropriate focus of the evaluation, is an ideal to strive for when the resources exist.

The main resource that may not be readily available is appropriate social science theory. Methods of articulating local program theory were developed in response to the apparent lack of well-developed social science theory (Trochim, 1985). Even when social science theories are available, their identification may be problematic. Relevant social science theories are difficult in part to identify because programs are rarely the incarnation of a single discipline. They manifest aspects of interest to many scientific fields, each of which may have different labels for the underlying variables. The constraints of both time and language make it difficult to search for applicable theories in all the potentially relevant fields. These constraints may be exacerbated by the lack of content knowledge of evaluators (Bickman, 1989). However, if not discipline-bound themselves, evaluators can act as liaisons between traditional social science fields by showing where theories from different disciplines converge in a single program.

The content knowledge of evaluators is one of several barriers to the use of program theory discussed by Bickman (1989). Other barriers, such as the cost of more extensive data collection and the lack of interest by evaluation clients in the theoretical basis for an evaluation, are also exacerbated when linking social science theory and program theory. These and other issues will continue to be addressed as theory-driven evaluations become the norm.

In the meantime, this chapter has shown that there is a middle ground between the reliance on inappropriate or poor social science theory and the uncritical use of program theory. Thoughtful linkage of program theory and social science theory can inform both program evaluation and social science research.

References

Bickman, L. "The Functions of Program Theory." In L. Bickman (ed.), *Using Program Theory in Evaluation*. New Directions for Program Evaluation, no. 33. San Francisco: Jossey-Bass, 1987.

Bickman, L. "Barriers to the Use of Program Theory." *Evaluation and Program Planning,* 1989, *12* (4), 387–390.

Campbell, D. T. "Relabeling Internal and External Validity for Applied Social Scientists." In W.M.K. Trochim (ed.), *Advances in Quasi-Experimental Design and Analysis*. New Directions for Program Evaluation, no. 31. San Francisco: Jossey-Bass, 1986.

Campbell, D. T., and Fiske, D. W. "Convergent and Discriminant Validation by Multitrait-Multimethod Matrix." *Psychological Bulletin,* 1959, *56,* 81–105.

Chen, H.-T. *Theory-Driven Evaluations*. Newbury Park, Calif.: Sage, 1990.

Chen, H.-T., and Rossi, P. H. "Evaluating with Sense: The Theory-Driven Approach." *Evaluation Review,* 1983, *7,* 283–302.

Chen, H.-T., and Rossi, P. H. "The Theory-Driven Approach to Validity." *Evaluaton and Program Planning,* 1987, *10,* 95–103.

Etzioni, E. *A Comparative Analysis of Complex Organizations*. New York: Free Press, 1975.

Finney, J. W., and Moos, R. H. "Theory and Method in Treatment Evaluation." *Evaluation and Program Planning,* 1989, *12* (4), 307–316.

Greene, J. C., Caracelli, V. J., and Graham, W. F. "Toward a Theory of Mixed-Method Evaluation Designs." *Educational Evaluation and Policy Analysis,* 1989, *11* (3), 255–274.

Leviton, L. C., and Hughes, E.F.X. "A Review and Synthesis of Research on the Utilization of Evaluations." *Evaluation Review,* 1981, *5,* 525–548.

McClintock, C. "Conceptual and Action Heuristics: Tools for the Evaluator." In L. Bickman (ed.), *Using Program Theory in Evaluation.* New Directions for Program Evaluation, no. 33. San Francisco: Jossey-Bass, 1987.

Riggin, L.J.C. "The Role of Program Theory in the Evaluation of an Employment Assistance Program." Unpublished manuscript, 1990.

Scheirer, M. A. "Program Theory and Implementation Theory: Implications for Evaluators." In L. Bickman (ed.), *Using Program Theory in Evaluation.* New Directions for Program Evaluation, no. 33. San Francisco: Jossey-Bass, 1987.

Trochim, W.M.K. "Pattern Matching, Validity, and Conceptualization in Program Evaluation." *Evaluation Review,* 1985, *9,* 575–604.

Trochim, W.M.K. "Pattern Matching and Program Theory." *Evaluation and Program Planning,* 1989, *12* (4), 355–366.

Wholey, J. "Evaluability Assessment: Developing Program Theory." In L. Bickman (ed.), *Using Program Theory in Evaluation.* New Directions for Program Evaluation, no. 33. San Francisco: Jossey-Bass, 1987.

Yin, R. K. *Case Study Research.* Newbury Park, Calif.: Sage, 1984.

Leslie J. C. Riggin is a social science analyst in the Program Evaluation and Methodology Division of the U.S. General Accounting Office, Washington, D.C.

INDEX

Administrators: activities related to information management by, 24; as applied theorists, 19-23; judging quality by, 28-32; methods of applied theorizing by, 23-24, 29-30, 32; strategies for applied theorizing of, 24-32
Adult day care (ADC), evaluation of, 73-88
Adult Day Care Assessment Procedure (ADCAP), 75-88
Adult Day Health Care Evaluation, 75
Aid to Families with Dependent Children (AFDC), evaluation of, 109-119
American Association of Retired Persons Andrus Foundation, 75
American Evaluation Association, 1
Applied theorizing: and administrative behavior, 20-23; administrative strategies for, 24-32; definition of, 19-20; judging the quality of, 28-32; methods of, 23-24, 29-30, 32
Argyris, C., 20, 23-24, 32

Ballassai, M. C., 94, 106
Baron, R. M., 40-41, 43, 48
Basic theorizing, definition of, 19-20
Bassett, R., 45, 46, 49
Baumrind, D., 40, 48-49
Bennis, W., 20, 25, 26, 32
Berk, R. A., 44, 50
Berwick, D. M., 64, 70
Bickman, L., 1, 4, 17, 37, 49, 53, 56, 66, 70, 71, 75, 89, 110, 119
Bingham, R. S., Jr., 64, 71
Blalock, H. M., 54, 56-57
Boyatzis, R. E., 25, 32
Brett, J. M., 41, 49
Bright Side Adult Day Care Center, 74
Brook, R., 62, 71
Brunnson, M., 26, 32
Bucuvales, M. J., 12, 18

Cacioppo, J. T., 45, 46, 49
Califano, J. A., 61, 71
Cameron, K. S., 25, 32
Campbell, D. T., 39, 45, 48, 49, 88, 89, 93, 100, 106, 115, 116, 119

Campione, P. F., 74, 89
Caracelli, V. J., 112, 120
Causal modeling: alternatives to, 38-39; criticism of, 40-41; path analysis as, 53; as process tracing, 40
Causative evaluations, 13-16
Causative theory, 10, 13-15
Chambers-Cook, K., 94, 107
Chen, H.-T., 1, 4, 10, 11, 12, 13, 14, 16, 17, 37, 38, 40, 43, 45, 49, 53, 57, 70, 71, 73, 89, 118, 119
Chodosh, H. L., 79-80, 89
Cialdini, R. B., 45, 46, 49
Cleary, P. D., 87, 89
Cochran, W. G., 39-40, 49
Cohen, M. D., 26, 32
Component approach, to evaluation, 66-67
Component Quality Checklist (CQC), 64, 67-69
Conceptual replication, 44-45
Conrad, K. J., 74-75, 76, 82, 83, 88, 89
Cook, T. D., 45, 46, 48, 49, 53, 57, 74, 88, 89
Cook, T. J., 43, 49
Cooper, J., 45, 49
Cordray, D. S., 15-16, 17, 38-39, 49
Costner, H. L., 38, 49
Cronbach, L. J., 16, 17, 42-43, 48, 49, 76, 85, 89
Cronkite, R. C., 88, 89
Crosse, S., 40, 42, 50, 61, 71

Davies, A. R., 62, 71, 87, 89, 90
Davis, J. E., 100, 106
Dawson, A. G., 94, 106
Deming, W. E., 64, 71
Descriptive theory, definition of, 7
Devine, E. C., 46, 49
Dewey, J., 8, 17, 61, 71
Donabedian, A., 62, 71, 87, 89
Duncan, O. D., 54, 57
Dunkle, J., 40, 42, 50, 61, 71
Dutton, J. M., 22, 32

Eash, M. J., 74, 89
Effective, definition of, 20

121

Elaboration: mediating variables as, 40–41; and mediation assessment, 43–47; with respect to cause, 43–45; in testing program theory, 39–40

Employment assistance program: conceptualizing the evaluation of, 110–112; evaluation context of, 109–110; interpreting the data on, 112–115; theory underlying, 111–113

Endogenous, definition of, 54

Etzioni, E., 115–118, 120

Evaluation: of function theories, 73–88; path analysis in, 53–56; of program characteristics, 75–77, 85–87; of program classification, 73–88; program theory and data from, 93–106; program theory and social science theory in, 109–119; of quality of programs, 61–70; tests of program theory as, 37–48; theory-driven, 13–16; value judgments in, 8–9. See also Tests of program theory

Evaluation and Program Planning, 1

Exogenous, definition of, 54

Fazio, R. H., 45, 49

Feldman, J., 56, 57

Fine, M., 42, 44, 50

Finney, J. W., 110, 118, 120

Fisher, Sir Ronald, 39

Fiske, D. W., 100, 106, 115, 119

Fitz-Gibbon, C. T., 53, 57

Flay, B., 88, 90

Freedman, D. A., 40, 50

Freeman, H. E., 30, 33

Function theories. See Program function theories

Goitein, B., 16, 17

Goldberg, R. S., 74, 89

Gomez, L. R., 94, 106

Goode, W. J., 8, 17

Graham, W. F., 112, 120

Greene, J. C., 112, 120

Gryna, F. M., Jr., 64, 71

Handicapped Children's Early Educational Programs, 64–65

Hanrahan, P., 75, 82, 83, 89

Hansberry Child Parent Center, 74

Head Start Program, 74

Hedrick, S. C., 75, 89

Hemple, C., 7, 17

Henke, C., 88, 90

House, E. R., 21, 33

Hughes, E. F., 26, 33, 110, 120

Hughes, S. L., 74, 75, 76, 82, 83, 89

Information management, administrative activities related to, 24

Integrative approaches, to program theory construction, 12–13

Inui, T. S., 75, 89

James, L. R., 41, 49

Japan, 64

Jöreskog, K. G., 78, 89

Judd, C. M., 40–41, 50

Juran, J. M., 64, 71

Kamberg, C. J., 62, 71

Kenny, D. A., 40–41, 43, 48, 50

Kerlinger, F. N., 7, 17

King, J., 94, 106

Koepke, D., 88, 90

Kolata, G., 41, 50

Krug, D. N., 94, 106

Kruskal, J. B., 97, 106

Land, K. C., 54, 57

Lave, C. A., 7, 8, 17

Lawndale Head Start, 74

Lemke, S., 75, 90

Lenihan, K. J., 44, 50

Leviton, L. C., 26, 33, 74, 89, 110, 120

Linn, R. L., 54, 57

Lipsey, M. W., 7–8, 16, 17, 40, 41, 42, 50, 61, 71, 73, 78, 90

Lohr, K., 62, 71

Lorenz, C. S., 94, 106

Low-balling, 45, 46

McClintock, C., 10–11, 21, 23, 30, 33, 53, 57, 93, 105, 106, 110, 120

McNeal, B. J., 87, 89

McTaggart, R., 21, 33

March, J. G., 7, 8, 17, 26, 32

Mark, M. M., 38, 40, 41, 43, 50

Marquart, J. M., 93, 95, 106

Mathison, S., 21, 33

Measurement. See Evaluation

Mediation: assessment of, 43–47; as elaboration, 40–41; and process manipulation, 41–43

Medicare, 79
Mikel, C. S., 94, 106
Milkovich, G. T., 94, 106
Miller, J. A., 45, 46, 49
Miller, T. I., 94, 106
Miller, T. Q., 74-75, 88, 89
Mintzberg, H., 22, 33
Moos, R. H., 15, 17, 75, 89, 90, 110, 118, 120
Morris, L. L., 53, 57
Multi-Attribute utility theory, 15
Multiphasic Environmental Assessment Procedure, 15, 75
Muro, E. S., 79-80, 89
Murray, S. L., 54, 55, 56, 57

National Institute of Adult Daycare, 75-76, 83
Nichols, J. G., 61, 71
Nisbett, R., 28, 33
Normative evaluations, 13-15
Normative theory, 13-15; definition of, 10
Nunnally, J. C., 75, 90

Olsen, J. P., 26, 32

Palmour, V. E., 94, 106
Patch-up designs, 15-16
Path analysis: cautions about, 56; definition of, 53-54; procedures, 53-55; uses for and examples of, 55-56
Pattern matching, 15-16, 78; across time, 46-47; background, 94-95; conclusions on, 103-106; definition of, 93; framework, 95-98; to link program theory and evaluation data, 93-106; measurement, 96, 98-101; outcome, 45, 96, 101-103; with respect to persons (or other units), 45-46; with respect to settings, 46; in testing program theory, 39-40
Patton, M. Q., 10-11, 18
Pedhazur, E. J., 56, 57
Perrow, C., 12, 18
PERT chart, 15
Philosophy, definition of, 74
Pirsig, R. M., 62, 71
Platt, J. R., 39, 50
Pollard, J., 16, 17, 40, 41, 42, 50, 61, 71, 73, 78, 90
Poole, W. K., 43, 49

Popper, K. R., 7, 18, 88, 90
Porac, J. E., 23-24, 33
Preschool programs, evaluation of quality of, 64-69
Prescriptive theory, 8-10
Pressman, J. L., 74, 90
Process manipulation: definition of, 41; as test of hypothesized mediators, 41-43
Program, definition of, 74
Program characteristics, measurement of, 75-77, 85-87
Program classification theories: evaluation of, 73-78; policy-relevant, 78-79; practice-relevant, 79-81; theoretical/observational, 81-85
Program function theories, evaluation of, 73-88
Program theory: and administrators as applied theorists, 19-32; approaches to, 10-13; and classification of programs, 73-88; construction of, 7-11; definitions of, 7-8, 9-10, 21; evaluation of, 37-48, 53-56, 61-70, 73-88, 93-106, 109-119; and function theories, 73-88; nature of, 7-10; and path analysis, 53-56; pattern matching and evaluation data of, 93-106; and quality measurement, 61-70; and social science theory, 109-119; subtheories of, 10; tests of, 37-48; and types of evaluation, 13-16
Project, definition of, 74
Purification approach, 43-44

Quality: criteria, 67-69; definitions of, 62-63; instrumentation, 69-70
Quality of programs, 61-70; applications of instrumentation on, 69-70; and component approach, 66-67; and criteria for quality, 67-69; and definition of quality, 62-63; emphasis on, 61-62; and improvement, 64; and preschool evaluation, 64-66

Reichardt, C. S., 43, 50, 53, 57
Resource theory, 8
Riggin, L.J.C., 115, 120
Roberts-Gray, C., 74, 76, 89, 90
Rockhart, J. F., 25, 33
Rosenbaum, P. R., 38, 39, 50
Ross, L., 28, 33

Rossi, P. H., 10, 11, 12, 16, 17, 30, 33, 37, 38, 40, 43, 44, 45, 49, 50, 53, 57, 73, 89, 118, 119
Rothman, M. L., 75, 89
Rutman, L., 10-11, 18

Salancik, G. R., 23-24, 33
Saxe, L., 42, 44, 50
Scheirer, M. A., 21, 33, 74, 90, 110, 120
Schön, D. A., 20, 21, 23-24, 28, 32, 33
Schwarz, P. A., 105, 107
Shadish, W. R., 53, 57, 74, 89
Side studies, 42, 44
Simborg, D. W., 88, 90
Smith, N. L., 54, 55-56, 57
Social science: approach to program theory construction, 11-12; and descriptive theory, 7; and social practice, 8
Social science theory: and program theory, 109-119; role of, in conceptualization, 115-116; role of, in interpretation, 116-118
Spaeth, J. L., 53-54, 56, 57
Sörbom, D., 78, 89
Srull, T. K., 47, 50
Stakeholders: approach to program theory construction, 10-11; multiple, 76
Standard Metropolitan Statistical Areas (SMSAs), 79
Standardized assessment instruments, and program quality, 69-70
Starbuck, W. H., 22, 32
Sternberg, R. J., 23-24, 33
Stobart, G., 40, 42, 50, 61, 71
Successful, definition of, 20

Tennessee Early Intervention Network for Children with Handicaps, 64-65
Tests of program theory, 37-48; elaboration in, 39-41, 43-47; methods for, 48; pattern matching in, 39-40, 43-47; prior recommendations about, 38-39; process manipulation in, 41-43
Theorizing: definition of, 19-20. See also Applied theorizing

Theory: definition of, 7, 74; methods for development of, 95-97. See also individual types
Theory-driven evaluations: analytical techniques for designing, 15-17; typology of, 13-15
Thibaut, J. W., 42, 50
Transition: definition of, 64; measuring, from preschool to school, 64-69
Transitional Aid Research Project (TARP), 44
Trochim, W.M.K., 10-11, 16, 18, 37, 39, 45, 50, 53, 57, 78, 90, 93, 94, 95, 107, 112, 115, 118, 119, 120

Valentine, K., 97, 107
Value judgments: and evaluations, 8-9; and prescriptive theory, 8
Veterans Affairs (VA), Department of, 75
Von Behren, R., 82, 83, 90
Vuori, H., 62, 71, 87, 90

Wagner, R. K., 23-24, 33
Walker, L., 42, 50
Ware, J., 87, 89, 90
Watts, C. A., 75, 89
Weick, K. E., 28, 33
Weiss, C. H., 12, 18
Weissert, W. G., 82, 90
Werts, C. E., 54, 57
Westinghouse Learning Corporation/ Ohio University, 74, 90
Whiting-O'Keefe, Q. E., 88, 90
Wholey, J. S., 8, 10-11, 12, 15, 18, 78, 90, 111, 120
Wildavsky, A. B., 74, 90
Wish, M., 97, 106
Wright, S., 54, 57
Wyer, R. S., 47, 50

Yin, R. K., 116, 120
Young, J. W., 56, 57
Youngblood, S. A., 94, 107

Zeffert, B., 79-80, 89
Zeisel, H., 44, 50

ORDERING INFORMATION

NEW DIRECTIONS FOR PROGRAM EVALUATION is a series of paperback books that presents the latest techniques and procedures for conducting useful evaluation studies of all types of programs. Books in the series are published quarterly in Fall, Winter, Spring, and Summer and are available for purchase by subscription as well as by single copy.

SUBSCRIPTIONS for 1990 cost $48.00 for individuals (a savings of 20 percent over single-copy prices) and $70.00 for institutions, agencies, and libraries. Please do not send institutional checks for personal subscriptions. Standing orders are accepted.

SINGLE COPIES cost $15.95 when payment accompanies order. (California, New Jersey, New York, and Washington, D.C., residents please include appropriate sales tax.) Billed orders will be charged postage and handling.

DISCOUNTS FOR QUANTITY ORDERS are available. Please write to the address below for information.

ALL ORDERS must include either the name of an individual or an official purchase order number. Please submit your order as follows:
  Subscriptions: specify series and year subscription is to begin
  Single copies: include individual title code (such as PE1)

MAIL ALL ORDERS TO:
  Jossey-Bass Inc., Publishers
  350 Sansome Street
  San Francisco, California 94104

FOR SALES OUTSIDE OF THE UNITED STATES CONTACT:
  Maxwell Macmillan International Publishing Group
  866 Third Avenue
  New York, New York 10022

OTHER TITLES AVAILABLE IN THE
NEW DIRECTIONS FOR PROGRAM EVALUATION SERIES
Nick L. Smith, *Editor-in-Chief*

PE46 Evaluating AIDS Prevention: Contributions of Multiple Disciplines,
Laura C. Leviton, Andrea M. Hegedus, Alan Kubrin

PE45 Evaluation and Social Justice: Issues in Public Education, *Kenneth A. Sirotnik*

PE44 Evaluating Training Programs in Business and Industry,
Robert O. Brinkerhoff

PE43 Evaluating Health Promotion Programs, *Marc T. Braverman*

PE42 International Innovations in Evaluation Methodology, *Ross F. Conner,
Michael Hendricks*

PE41 Evaluation and the Federal Decision Maker, *Gerald L. Barkdoll,
James B. Bell*

PE40 Evaluating Program Environments, *Kendon J. Conrad,
Cynthia Roberts-Gray*

PE39 Evaluation Utilization, *John A. McLaughlin, Larry J. Weber,
Robert W. Covert, Robert B. Ingle*

PE38 Timely, Lost-Cost Evaluation in the Public Sector, *Christopher G. Wye,
Harry P. Hatry*

PE37 Lessons from Selected Program and Policy Areas, *Howard S. Bloom,
David S. Cordray, Richard J. Light*

PE36 The Client Perspective on Evaluation, *Jeri Nowakowski*

PE35 Multiple Methods in Program Evaluation, *Melvin M. Mark,
R. Lance Shotland*

PE34 Evaluation Practice in Review, *David S. Cordray, Howard S. Bloom,
Richard J. Light*

PE33 Using Program Theory in Evaluation, *Leonard Bickman*

PE32 Measuring Efficiency: An Assessment of Data Envelopment Analysis,
Richard H. Silkman

PE31 Advances in Quasi-Experimental Design and Analysis,
William M. K. Trochim

PE30 Naturalistic Evaluation, *David D. Williams*

PE29 Teaching of Evaluation Across the Disciplines, *Barbara Gross Davis*

PE28 Randomization and Field Experimentation, *Robert F. Boruch,
Werner Wothke*

PE27 Utilizing Prior Research in Evaluation Planning, *David S. Cordray*

PE26 Economic Evaluations of Public Programs, *James S. Catterall*